D0105362

63166   Legal Almanac Series No. 14

COPYRIGHT, PATENTS AND TRADEMARKS:
The Protection of Intellectual and Industrial Property

by Richard Wincor and Irving Mandell

*This Legal Almanac has been revised
by the Oceana Editorial Staff*

Irving J. Sloan
General Editor

**1980
Oceana Publications, Inc.
Dobbs Ferry, New York**

Library of Congress Cataloging in Publication Data

Wincor, Richard & Mandell, Irving
   Copyright, patents, and trademarks.

   (Legal almanac series; no. 14)
   Includes index.
   1. Copyright—United States.   2. Patent laws and
legislation—United States.   3. Trade-marks—United
States.   I. Title.
KF2980.S55   346.7304'8   80-17681
ISBN 0-379-11138-1

© Copyright 1980 by Oceana Publications, Inc.

Manufactured in the United States of America

TABLE OF CONTENTS

Chapter I

HISTORICAL BACKGROUND—COPYRIGHT LAW

Literary piracy, while less romantic than its nautical counterpart, has the advantage of being infinitely more in fashion. The Jolly Roger has been hauled down. In its place, as the term "piracy" is used today, we have the solemn trappings of respectability. A modern buccaneer may lunch at Sardi's and browse afterwards in the Public Library. Despite this, his offense (which is simply what we used to call "cribbing") is far more villainous than robbery at sea. This is because it takes from a man what he has least of, picking not alone his pocket, but his brains.

Plagiarism of all sorts has a distinguished history. It begins in ancient times, when there were no copyright laws, and continues into our own day in which the development of motion pictures, television and other forms of transmission has greatly increased the value and the vulnerability of works of art. In some degree the law has kept pace with the new art forms. In the United States at present there is a dual system of protection for your work. Before you publish it (and what constitutes publication will be considered later) you need do absolutely nothing at all; if anyone steals from it you can sue him, since unpublished works are protected by the great corpus of Anglo-American common law developed over the course of centuries in the courts. This automatic protection of unpublished works is called common law copyright. Once you publish, however, you must comply with certain formalities required by the Copyright Act. This second phase, statutory copyright, is the result of legislative enactment. One is the creature of tradition, the other of Congress. The rights you have under the two systems are not the same. How this came to be, and what significance

1

it has, are the subjects of one of the most portentous and fantastic debates of all time.

The proposition that no one else may copy one's creation is relatively new. Quite obviously the author has complete ownership of his physical manuscript, just as he has complete ownership of his desk, his chair, his headache powders. But what about the contents of his manuscript? These are intangible; they are harder to conceive as a property susceptible of being owned. For this reason the history of authors,' artists,' and composers' rights is a chronicle of misfortunes. The creative artist is one of history's favorite whipping-boys, and his contribution to society is too often thought of as less sacred than the products of the workbench and conveyor belt. These unhappy notions have retarded the promotion of culture with deadlier thoroughness than those other favorites, the pillory and the burning of the books. All, in fact, have their origin in the same impulse.

The initial problem appears quite simple: for how long, if ever, does a creative artist own all the rights in his creation? Among those who have attempted answers, with varying degrees of vituperation, are Milton, Swift, Hume, Addison and Steele, Lord Mansfield, Johnson, Boswell, Macaulay, Arnold and Disraeli in England; Madison, both Websters, and many others in the United States. The question became crucial with the development of printing in the sixteenth century. It remains to this day a subject of debate and UNESCO, whose mission is to promote culture through the free exchange of ideas, has created a special Copyright Committee for the study of this problem Our Department of State is concerned with it. Authors' societies, producers, typographical unions and the Copyright Office in Washington have a multitude of views. In this field, discard is the norm.

ORIGINS OF COPYRIGHT

In the English-speaking countries, according to an ancient legend, copyright was first enforced in the year

567 A.D. In that year the ecclesiast Columba made a copy of a psalter in the possession of his teacher Finnian. A controversy arose and the cause was adjudicated by King Diarmud in the Halls of Tara, who held in favor of the plaintiff Finnian with the phrase, "To every cow her calf." Despite this small unpleasantness Columba shortly afterwards was made a saint in honor of his splendid efforts in converting the Pictish Druids. The phrase "to every cow her calf" was also canonized, though in a different way. It is quoted in nearly every work on copyright, having as it does the kind of agricultural charm that appeals to city lawyers. The phrase, however, has a distinct significance. It recognizes, perhaps for the first time on record, the existence of such a thing as literary property.

For centuries thereafter the status of literary property is shrouded in British fog. Presumably the traditional common law of the realm protected new forms of property as well as old, creations of the mind along with acquisitions of the hand. No one knows. Whatever may have been the case, an alarming thing happened in the sixteenth century. The New Learning, so called, menaced both church and state with heresy. At that time the celebrated Stationers' Company of London, a publishers' association, held one of the royal patents without which it was forbidden to print books for sale in Great Britain. Accordingly the authorities availed themselves of the company files to keep track of heretical authors, who might then be put in the stocks. Sir Edward Arber, who compiled the transcript of the Stationers' Registers in 1875, had this to say about it: "As books became more and more a power, and therefore dangerous things unless fully authorized by the Ordinary, the book entries became a permission and imprimateur rather than a cash receipt." A series of Star Chamber decrees made things even more unpleasant for the author. Milton's *Areopagitica* was the most famous protest against these sorry practices. Copyright registration and deposit are defended nowadays on the ground that they enrich the national library with good books. Be that as it may, the formalities of official copyright had a bad beginning. Those old files of the Stationers' Company· are a monument to the absurd pretenses of censorship.

THE STATUTE OF ANNE

Literary piracy continued to plague authors where censorship left off. By the turn of the eighteenth century it was becoming a national outrage. Swift, Addison and Steele and certain publishers who owned copyrights told friends in Parliament that the traditional common law remedies were not enough. Accordingly in 1709, when Anne was Queen of England, an Act of Parliament[1] was passed giving special protection for fourteen years against the piracy of published works. Its sponsors little dreamed that it would set off a debate destined to reverberate throughout that century and up to the present day. That, however, is what happened. In the case called *Donaldson* v. *Becket*,[2] an interpretation of Anne's Act by the House of Lords in 1774 caught the unsuspecting author with his quill down and set the stage for a supreme comedy of errors.

THE GREAT DEBATE

A great debate began when Donaldson, a Scotch publisher, brought out an edition of James Thomson's *The Seasons* without the owner's consent. *The Seasons* had been published and then protected for the prescribed term by the Statute of Anne. That term, however, had now expired and most British authors and publishers assumed that the work was still protected by common law as it was before publication. The defendant maintained that the Statute of Anne replaced and destroyed the old common law protection; that while such protection would be perpetual, protection under the Statute of Anne was limited to a term of years, which had run out. Anybody, then, could publish *The Seasons* as he pleased. Furthernore, said counsel for the defendant, common law copyright never existed anyway, even before publication. At

4

this all of literary England chose sides and a controversy raged. Authors, lawyers, churchmen, nearly everyone who read and thought plunged headfirst into the affray. The kingdom was deluged with pamphlets inventing the most ingenious and metaphysical arguments to prove that there was or was not such a thing as perpetual "Literary Property." Every man was his own Aquinas. A clear statement of the author's position, which was doomed, is that of Hargrave writing at Lincoln's Inn in 1774: "I argue that the publication instead of destroying or diminishing the brief right of the author to the sole printing and selling of his works tends to render that right more firm and actually introduces many and additional pretensions for asserting it."

It was in 1774 that the case went before the House of Lords as the supreme judicial body of Great Britain. On January 29 Dr. Johnson wrote to Boswell in Scotland, saying, "The question of Literary Property is this day before the Lords. Murphy drew up the Appellant's case, that is, the plea against the perpetual right." The giant's lines convey a portly rustle of excitement. When the Lords assembled, all eyes were on Lord Mansfield, the most eminent of jurists, who had declared himself in favor of the perpetual right in earlier decisions. At that time it was considered bad etiquette for a peer to support his own lower court decisions in the House of Lords. Unfortunately for authors Lord Mansfield was afflicted with good manners and kept silence. As a result the forces on the other side carried the day. One of their champions was Sir John Dalrymple who argued that publication destroyed the rights at common law, saying, "Now an ogle is a ladies' own whilst private, but if she ogles publicly, they are everyone's property." This unrealistic and ungrammatical quip led the peers into a receptive frame of mind for Lord Camden's tirade against the monopoly of publishers and authors. *Donaldson* v. *Becket* went for the defendant. The judges' vote held that literary property existed at common law but that once an author published, he was protected only for the term specified in the Statute of Anne, and not a minute longer. In the next century a parallel situation arise in the United States and our Supreme Court followed the English decision with proper reverence for authority.[3] Thus a decision by the Lords in 1774 determined the sage principles that relate to motion pictures, mechanical records and television in our own day.

One thing which the peers did not accomplish was the ending of the great debate. It raged on, sometimes academically, sometimes in connection with new copyright bills. Macaulay said that copyright was a monopoly; Herbert Spencer said that it was not. In 1879 a New York lawyer with the soporific name of Drone chose to reopen the entire question of Literary Property, saying, "Its ownership like that of all property is transferred only with the consent of the author. It is no more lost by publication than the ownership of land is lost by a grant of the privilege of hunting, felling timber, or digging minerals within its borders." Drone, however, lived and wrote too late. It may be that some policy against "monopoly" might have caught up with authors if the House of Lords had not, but that notion is disposed of by a witty member of a later British Parliament, Mr. Augustine Birrell, who wrote; "But how annoying, how distressing, to have evolution artificially arrested and so interesting a question stifled by an ignorant legislature, set in motion not by an irate populace clamoring for cheap books (as a generation later they were to clamor for cheap gin) but by the authors and their proprietors, the booksellers."

PUBLIC BENEFIT

It cannot be maintained, however, that the perpetual rights of authors were destroyed simply by a single determination in the House of Lords. The public may be less concerned with cheap books than with cheap gin, but the public was nevertheless the chief figure in this chronicle. The pressure felt through its aspirations, its demand for the good things of life, brought about a limitation on the rights of creative artists. It was against the public interest that a masterpiece should be susceptible of permanent monopoly; at the same time it is sheer banditry to take away from someone that which he creates in the exercise of his own talents. Fortunately, the two interests can be reconciled. Our present copyright laws, with all their flaws, are evidence that this is true. They take away the author's perpetual rights after he publishes his work but they grant him a new set of rights for a term of years to encourage him through rewarding his self-interest. This in turn redounds to the general welfare. Dr. Johnson stated the matter aptly in these terms:

"For the general good of the world, therefore, whatever valuable work has once been created by the author, and issued out by him should be understood as no longer in his power, but as belonging to the public; at the same time the author is entitled to receive an adequate reward."

Legislative history in the United States affords the clearest proof that public benefit is the true theory of our copyright laws. Twelve of the original thirteen states passed copyright acts before the Federal Constitution was adopted. The titles of these acts were in nearly all cases phrased in terms of the general welfare. The Connecticut Statute was called "An Act for the encouragement of Literature and Genius." New York passed "An Act to promote Literature"; and so go the others. Their preambles, or general statements of purpose, are in the same vein. The Massachusetts Act is a good example:

"Whereas the Improvement of Knowledge, the Progress of Civilization, the public Weal of the Community, and the Advancement of Human Happiness, greatly depend on the efforts of learned and ingenious Persons in the various Arts and Sciences: as the principal Encouragement such Persons can have to make great and beneficial Exertions of this Nature, must exist in the legal Security of the Fruits of their Study and Industry to themselves ,and as such Security is one of the natural Rights of all Men,

7

there being no Property more peculiarly a Man's own than that which is produced by the Labour of his Mind:

"Therefore, to encourage learned and ingenious Persons to write useful Books for the Benefit of Mankind,

"Be it enacted . . ."

This extraordinary passage reflects the paradox implicit in all copyright protection. Creations of the mind are peculiarly a man's own; yet in the public interest they must be taken away after publication, with proper rewards to the author, however, to encourage him to create more works of art for the public.

In our Constitution the concepts of twelve states have been made into a statement of national policy. Article I, Section 8 proclaims:

"The Congress shall have power . . .

"To promote the Progress of Science and useful Arts, by securing for limited Times to Authors and Inventors the exclusive Right to their respective Writings and Discoveries."

With this authorization the Congress has passed successive Copyright Acts. The House Report accompanying the present Act, which dates back to 1909, reaffirms the purpose of such legislation in these words: "Not primarily for the benefit of the author, but primarily for the benefit of the public, such rights are given."

This is the history of our dual system of copyright. Under the common law one's property in his work is unqualified and perpetual. It may be that common law copyright will be superseded, as in England now, by statutory provisions regarding unpublished as well as published works. One reason this may happen is the public interest in the unpublished works of deceased authors such as Mark Twain, which are withheld from it by the absolutism of common law protection. In the case of *Chamberlain* v. *Feldman*,[4] the plaintiffs, as successor trustees under the will of Samuel L. Clemens (Mark Twain) sued to restrain the defendant Feldman from publishing, producing, or reproducing a story by Clemens entitled "A Murder, A

Mystery, and A Marriage." This story was written by Twain in 1876 with the plan of enlisting the aid of other famous authors, such as Bret Harte, each to write his own final chapter for the work. Twain submitted the manuscript to William Dean Howells, editor of the *Atlantic Monthly*, but the plan fell through. When Twain died in 1910 the manuscript was not found among his effects and had never been published anywhere by anyone. In 1945 the defendant Feldman purchased it at an auction sale in New York of rare books that had belonged to Dr. James Brentano Clemens (no kin of Mark Twain). Eager to publish it, Mr. Feldman sought permission of the trustees under the author's will, and being refused, went ahead with the publication anyway. The trustees' suit to enjoin such publication met with final success in 1950 when the Court of Appeals in the State of New York agreed that Mark Twain had never parted with his common law copyright, which is a thing separate from physical possession of the manuscript. The court hinted that it had doubts as to the advisability of "permitting literary flowers so to blush unseen," and that it would prefer the work to go into the public domain for all to enjoy. This result, however, could be accomplished only by the Legislature. Accordingly the unhappy Feldman was enjoined from publishing the work.

At this time, therefore, the common law still governs and protects unpublished works. After publication one's work is given only limited protection and solely on condition of compliance with the Copyright Act. This requirement we have seen, had its origins in censorship and was subsequently confirmed in a celebrated debate influenced by the growing pressure of public interest in the arts. The public interest in its turn became paramount, and nowadays is the true fabric of Anglo-American copyright law.

Piracy, however, still menaces the arts. The opportunities are endless, the booty unprecedented. It may appear that this account of events past is impractical in a world of pirates, but quite the opposite is true. The history of legal weapons is a guide in their proper use. So armed, you are on the way to catching the would-be pirate in his crime, and making him haul down his flag.

1. 8 Anne ch. 19 (1710)
2. 4 Burrows 2303 (1774)
3. Wheaton v. Peters, 8 Pet. 591 (1834)
4. 300 N. Y. 135 (1950)

Chapter II

LEGAL DOCTRINE OF THE PUBLIC DOMAIN

The public domain is the People's bailiwick. In it are those creations of the human intellect which are owned by nobody; they are the common property of the world and can be used or reproduced by all. Thus the public domain includes most of the world's masterpieces. Falstaff is there, waiting perpetually to be revived without royalties to his maker. Bruege's Icarus recounts the pathos of man's aspirations on museum postcards. Mozart's "Hunt" quartet can be performed by the local chamber music society, free of charge. Material in the public domain being unprotected by law, its reproduction is in no way piracy. Of course there is always the possibility that arrangements, abridgments, or other special versions of works in the public domain may have enough originality for ownership by someone living. Such embellishments can be copyrighted, but the original work remains the property of everyone. Most of the world's treasures, then, are in the public domain.

There is nothing surprising in the fact that Shakespeare's plays are not "copyrighted." To those of you who write, however, it may come as a surprise to learn that your idea, your theme, format, plot, setting, and probably your characters and title are also in the public domain. They are not yours because they are incapable of being owned. The person who copies them acts fully within his rights. If this seems outrageous, remember that each of the elements cited is bound to be unoriginal; only the specific treatment given it can be unique, and accordingly, this specific treatment is all that the law protects. If these principles were understood, the allegations of piracy today would generally be on a higher level.

The enormity of the public domain cannot be over-emphasized. Suppose, for example, you had a bright idea for an advertising scheme and revealed it without agreement as to reward. Suppose further you conceived a design for a new building, or the rules for a game, or a scientific theory that would shake the world. In any such case your idea would be protected only by silence, not by law. There is no property in an idea until its reduction to concrete and tangible form. The idea for a new building must become an architectural sketch; the scientific theory must be developed in a learned monograph. Until such time, anyone else can use your idea to his own profit if he learns about it. So universally is this established that lawsuits for theft of an "idea" no longer clutter up the court. Instead nowadays the victim always founds his action on the breach of an implied contract to pay for disclosure of an original idea or abuse of a fiduciary relation, which are different things from copyright. The results, however, tend to be just as unfortunate. Contracts to pay for ideas are hard to get and harder to prove. Accordingly the next time you have a valuable idea, such as writing about life in an opium den, keep it to yourself and write it first. Then you can show it to anyone because the text, as it takes on specific form, will be protected by common law. Others can thereafter write up their own experiences in opium dens, but your version must not be copied. The same principles apply to "information." Scholars may well consider the words of an Alabama court:

"It must be understood, however, that where the information is accessible to others there can be no ownership of the information itself, but only of the memorial thereof —the *collective form* into which it has been cast by the labor of the claimant."[5]

Themes

By the same token a theme or motif in art is also in the public domain. Thus a drama on dual personality has been held not to infringe a copyrighted play dealing with the same subject matter.[6] In another case a copyrighted story about wild horses was held not to have been infringed by a motion picture with the same theme, which the court defined as "the underlying thought which impresses the reader of a literary production, or the text of a discourse."[7] Similarly it was held that a play called "Depends On The Woman" was not infringed by the movie operetta "I Dream Too Much," the court saying, "The only possible similarity between the works is that of the theme, which is not subject to exclusive copyright."[8] Only the means of expressing a theme or idea can be protected. In a famous case one judge put the matter in these words:

"Just as a patent affords protection only to the means of reducing an inventive idea to practice, so the copyright law protects the means of expressing an idea; and it is as near the whole truth as generalization can usually reach that, if the same idea can be expressed in a plurality of totally different manners, a plurality of copyrights may result, and no infringement will exist."[9]

Plots

Plots are as incapable of ownership as ideas or themes. In fact one critic, Polti, writes that only thirty-six dramatic plots exist. The courts have gone even further, saying that specific incidents, effects and atmosphere, even similar phrases in dialogue were not copyrightable. Some well-known plays have been involved in these lawsuits: "Death Takes a Holiday,"[10] "They Knew What They Wanted,"[11] and "Of Thee I Sing"[12] are some of them. In the last case, "Of Thee I Sing" was held not to infringe "U.S.A. With Music" and the court, apparently annoyed by the unfounded claims of piracy, delivered itself of an unkind but pointed reflection. "In this cause," the opinion reads, "as is usual in plagiarism causes, obscurity is taking a long shot at success."

The Thing of Value

By this time it should be clear that a good portion of

what you thought was yours is everybody's. Disillusioning as this may be, it is the basis of wise ownership of creative works. When you realize how vast is the public domain you can appreciate the absurdity of the phrase "he stole my story," in the majority of cases. In all fairness there have recently been indications of some inroads on the public domain. Particularly in two cases a court went very far toward protecting the theme or format of one work from being copied in another. How far this unorthodoxy may spread is anybody's guess. The cases referred to were decided in California, where the common law relating to unpublished material has been codified. Factors such as these make it difficult to know error from trend.

Nevertheless, the two cases are worth noting. In one, *Golding* v. *RKO Pictures, Inc.*,[13] the plaintiff was co-author of "The Man and His Shadow," a play never published or dedicated to the public. The plaintiff submitted his play to RKO's producer who kept it six weeks and returned it. Subsequently the defendant RKO produced a motion picture called "The Ghost Ship" and this action followed. A judgment for $25,000 was awarded plaintiff and was affirmed by the California Supreme Court in an extraordinary decision.

Plaintiff's play had, as its central core, a sea captain accused of murder by a passenger, the captain's attempt to convince the crew that the passenger suffered from hallucinations, and his final breakdown and madness through knowledge that the murder would be discovered. Defendant's motion picture was similar but changed the voyage to a pleasure cruise and the captain to an imposter hating his former employer, and made other changes in minor characters and incidents. In the most unorthodox but practical terms the court declared:

"Literary property in the fruits of a writer's creative endeavor extends to the full scope of his inventiveness. This may well include, in the case of a stage play or moving picture scenario, the entire plot, the unique dialogue, the fundamental emotional appeal or theme of the story, or merely certain novel sequences or combinations of otherwise hackneyed elements. It is, however, only the product of the writer's creative mind which is protectable."

The court based its decision here on appropriation of the central dramatic situation as the *thing of value*. Testimony that such was the actual thing of value was given by a studio story editor who described how material is trimmed to meet budgets so that the basic situation which remains (here a psychological one) is the item to be protected. It was of no consequence that the plot was old and obtainable elsewhere. Plaintiff's property lay in the "dramatic core" of the play. (The viewpoint of the ordinary observer is used as a test for similarity but not as a test of originality or protectability, which is the court's province; hence similarity is tested by standards of the ordinary observer looking at the protected portion as delineated by the court.) One judge dissented on the ground that there is no property in such "hackneyed" situations.

In a second case decided the same day, *Stanley v. Columbia Broadcasting System, Inc.*,[14] the same court passed upon an action to recover on an alleged implied agreement of the defendant to pay the plaintiff for a radio program which the plaintiff claimed to have originated. The plaintiff alleged originating and causing to be written a radio script, "Walter Wanger Presents" and a program format "Preview Parade" or "Hollywood Preview" to give the public a voice in selecting stories and stars for motion pictures. The plaintiff recorded his material and presented script, format, and records to the defendant for purchase or license under an implied agreement to pay their reasonable value. This was during 1942-44. In 1945 the defendant CBS produced a radio program called "Hollywood Preview." The plaintiff's program proposed a "theatre of the air" where motion picture scenarios were introduced by a celebrity who solicited the public to write in their views and suggest casting, with prizes for the best letter. The defendant's program contained these elements with its central feature, not so much audience selection of scripts as simulation of opening night atmosphere, although suggestions for casting were accepted and voting for stories was made a special six-weeks' feature. A jury found that there was substantial similarity between the two programs and the plantiff was awarded judgment for $35,000.

Affirming the Superior Court, L. A. County, the California Supreme Court stated that protection of ideas by their originator depended on (1) whether the idea was novel, (2) reduced to concrete form prior to appropriation by defendant, to whom the originator had disclosed it, (3) whether circumstances of disclosure indicated expectation of compensation for use. Infringement is a question for the triers of fact, and there was evidence here to support the jury's finding of substantial similarity where access gave an opportunity to copy.

What is worth while noting, however, is that the court found protectable elements in the original treatment of old plots, stating in bold terms:

". . . when all these elements are joined to make one idea for a radio program, it is the combination which is new and novel."

One judge analyzed the law as follows:

"An author who takes existing materials from sources common to all writers, arranges and combines them in a new form, giving them an application unknown before, is entitled to a copyright, notwithstanding the fact that he may have borrowed much of his materials and ideas from others, provided they are assembled in a different manner and combined for a different purpose, and his plan and arrangement are a real improvement upon existing modes; for the labor of making these selections, arrangements and combinations has entailed the exercise of skill, discretion, and creative effort."

Another judge, concurring, found substantial similarity between all main elements of the two programs, and every opportunity for piracy, so that his sole question was fitness for protectability. Unlike the *Golding* case, he said, more than the "central core" had been reproduced; and the crucial problem, whether the plaintiff's plan was an "original" product of his mind he answered affirmatively, declaring that the plaintiff suggested a novel adaptation and application of the audience participation idea.

A third judge, dissenting, considered the plaintiff's program element by element to show lack of originality and added that in combination they were equally unoriginal. Using the same key question of protectability, this judge asserted that the plaintiff's program was not infringed because it was not susceptible of ownership.

Thus in a fateful day the California Supreme Court, by split decisions, did its bit in disturbing the old notions of what lies in the public doman. Dramatic cores and program formats, in the traditonal vew, were no one's property.

Despite the California holdings it is still safe to assume that ideas, theme, format, plot, setting, and their judicial synonyms are not copyrightable. The same is true of published names and titles, which are a little different however, and ought to be considered separately.

Characters

An author's characters are actually his greatest problem. The manner of their delineation is perhaps a real test of artistic quality, and the language in the latter cases suggests that an author's characters may be protected if sufficiently individualized. In this connection some comments by a British court are worth noting:

"But if a character is, so to speak, 'lifted,' or one or two single situations, the problem becomes more difficult. Can it be said that in relation to performing right, and to that right alone, individual ideas can be protected under the Act? If, for nstance, we found a modern playwright creating a character as distinctive and remarkable as Falstaff or as Tartuffe, or (to come to a recent classic) as Sherlock

Holmes, would it be an infringement if another writer, one of the servile flock of imitators, were to borrow the idea and to make use of an obvious copy of the original? I should hesitate a long time before I came to such a conclusion. I should feel the same doubt in reference to the taking of an ingenious situation, for instance an improvement on the screen scene in 'The School of Scandal' or a new device for turning the tables on the villain provided that it was an unimportant incident in the play. Anyone may introduce into his show Harlequin, Pierrot, Columbine and Pantaloon, or their modern and more complex exemplars, just as anyone may use in the invention of a machine levers, toothed wheels, racks and pinions, connecting rods and the other well-known mechanical parts. It is the use which the author of play or film makes of these well-known characters in composing his dramatic scenes that the Court has to consider in a case of alleged infringement; in other words, the plaintiff has to show that the combination or series of dramatic events in the infringing work have been taken from the like situations in the plaintiff's work . . . To hold the contrary would be to give a producer or novelist not only a monopoly in an idea, but a monopoly in an idea without the merit of novelty. The plaintiff, in order to prove his right, must at least establish that he is the *author* of the character or the idea in some sense of the word."[15]

The most pointed American pronouncement on this subject was made in connection with an infringement suit that involved "Abie's Irish Rose." In holding that it was not infringed by "The Cohens and the Kelleys," despite the appearance in both plays of elemental Irish and Jewish stock characters nonplussed by intermarriage, the court declared:

"If 'Twelfth Night' were copyrighted, it is quite possible that a second composer might so closely imitate Sir Toby Belch or Malvolio as to infringe, but it would not be enough that for one of his characters he cast a riotous knight who kept wassail to the discomfort of the household,

18

or a vain and foppish steward who became amorous of his mistress. These would be more than Shakespeare's 'ideas' in the plan, as little capable of monopoly as Einstein's Doctrine of Relativity, or Darwin's theory of the Origin of Species. It follows that the less developed the characters, the less they can be copyrighted; that is the penalty an author must bear for marking them too indistinctly . . .

"There are but four characters common to both plays, the lovers and the fathers. The lovers are so faintly indicated as to be no more than stage properties. They are loving and fertile; that is really all that can be said of them, and anyone else is quite within his rights if he puts loving and fertile lovers in a play of his own, whenever he gets the chance."[16]

In a sense then, the author's property in his characters is a measure of his own ability. This is certainly fair enough; it makes ownership the reward for genius. If your characters are undistinguished they must fall, with the other stock elements, into the public domain. If they are genuine human beings artistically portrayed, you own them.

Taboo

The most curious item not capable of being copyrighted is immoral or obscene matter. This taboo is conceptually sound since the public interest, which is the basis of our copyright laws, is opposed to the dissemination of such matter. Nevertheless, an obscene work can hardly be said to fall into the public domain for anyone to use. Uncopyrightable, just as ideas and plots are, the consequences of its being so are different. It differs even more from defamatory matter, for while our libel and slander laws originated in the public interest in preventing duels, works violating these laws are not uncopyrightable merely because they create liability. Defamation, then, is a subject apart from copyright. Obscenity is not. Obscene works resemble stock elements in belonging to no one; instead of falling into the public domain, however, they are consigned to a public limbo of perpetual disuse. This unique feature is easily explained as a practical matter. Obscene works are forbidden by state penal statutes. What constitutes obscenity, then, is a question largely answered in terms of statutes reflecting community morals at a given date.

It is a far cry from Dickens' "D--n it, Sir!" to Faulkner's heroine who is ravished with a corncob. The present view of immoral and obscene matter is set forth in one of the book-banning cases, in Pennsylvania.[17] Here the court held that certain booksellers did not violate the state law by possessing the following books with intent to sell them: The Studs Lonigan Trilogy (*Young Lonigan, The Young Manhood of Studs Lonigan, Judgment Day*), by James T. Farrell; *A World I Never Made*, by James T. Farrell; *Sanctuary*, by William Faulkner; *Wild Palms*, by William Faulkner; *God's Little Acre*, by Erskine Caldwell; *End as a Man*, by Calder Willingham and *Never Love a Stranger*, by Harold Robbins. Reviewing prior cases the court declared:

"From all these cases the modern rule is that obscenity is measured by the erotic allurement upon the average modern reader; that the erotic allurement of a book is measured by whether it is sexually impure—i.e., pornographic, 'dirt for dirt's sake,' a calculated incitement to sexual desire—or whether it reveals an effort to reflect life, including its dirt, with reasonable accuracy and balance; and that mere coarseness or vulgarity is not obscenity."

The court noted that Holmes' famous "clear and present danger" test of free speech was inapplicable to obscenity:

"The public does not read a book and simultaneously rush by the hundreds into the streets to engage in orgiastic riots." The dirt for dirt's sake test for considering the entire work is consistent with Macaulay's statement:

"We find it difficult to believe that in a world so full of temptations as this, any gentleman, whose life would have been virtuous if he had not read Aristophanes and Juvenal, will be made vicious by reading them."

The book-banning cases should be distinguished from other instances of censorship that provide no standard for copyright problems. For example, *Curley*, a film designed for juvenile market, was banned in Memphis. *Curley*, is the story of michievous schoolboys and a new teacher. The boys fail in their attempts to upset her with ants, frogs and automobile smoke. She wins their affection with good looks and good sportsmanship. At the end she is victorious in a boxing exhibition with the school bully. It would seem that no film could be less objectionable. *Curley* was banned solely because it allowed Negro and white children playing together. Nevertheless, the Memphis standards are no part of the copyright law. Copyright can be acquired in works portraying social equality. Only dirt for dirt's sake is taboo.

Infringement

This survey of the public domain raises a fundamental question. What constitutes the borderline between the public domain and private property? Generally anyone may copy such stock elements as plot, theme and setting, but not the specific form or language by which these elements are given original treatment. The latter is private property; whoever goes there commits infringement. And the border is not easily marked.

Infringement or piracy is substantial copying of protected material without the owner's consent. There is no absolute test and there never will be; you must simply consult a copyright lawyer if you think you have a case. Nevertheless if you consider infringement as the borderline and have a general idea what lies on each side, you know as much as anyone can know about it in advance. The intent to infringe is unnecessary to the offense. Whether or not one work is stolen from another depends on the particular facts in each case. The greater problem, and the one which this survey of the public domain is meant to illustrate, is whether the thing supposedly infringed is capable of being infringed at all by being susceptible of ownership. Thereby hangs the tale, and the courts are not always aware of it. Frequently their discussions of infringement make up a pageant of prolix evasions enlivened occasionally by a split infinitive. When they are precise, they come back usually to what I have been urging as the real problem not piracy, but copyright; not whether there was theft, but whether there could be ownership. Thus in holding that Holmes' "Autocrat of the Breakfast Table" was not copyrightable because of its earlier serial publication in a magazine, the court declared:

"The right thus secured by the copyright act is not a right to the use of certain words, because they are the common property of the human race, and are as little susceptible of private appropriation as air and sunlight; nor is it the right to ideas alone, since in the absence of means of communicating them they are of value to no one, but the author. But the right is to that arrangement of words which the author has selected to express his ideas."[18]

What it all means is that the borderline of infringement is fixed by the limits of the public domain. Where infringement is charged, the court or jury may study both works, phrase by phrase, line by line or stroke by stroke, to see whether substantial copying in fact took place. Paraphrase as well as verbatim copying may constitute infringement. That the real question, though, should be whether the supposedly infringed work is really in the public domain is quite logical in view of what was suggested in the previous chapter. There I contended that public benefit was the true theory of American copyright law. This being so, nothing can be infringed that belongs to the public.

Access

For this reason in infringement cases the plaintiff must prove that the defendant had "access" to the work allegedly infringed. If the defendant produces something identical with the plaintiff's work by mere chance, there is no infringement. As one judge phrased it:

22

"Borrowed the work must indeed not be, for a plagirist is not himself *pro tanto* an author; but if by some magic a man who had never known it were to compose anew Keat's Ode on a Grecian Urn, he would be an 'author' and, if he copyrighted it, others might not copy that poem, though they might of course copy Keat's."[19] Needless to say, the courts do not generally believe in magic. Hence this language is no invitation to copy another's work and then claim never to have seen it.

Fair Use

Another manifestation of the public's interest is the so-called doctrine of Fair Use. This refers simply to the right of making limited and acknowledged quotations from another's published work for purposes of criticism or comment. The comment may be as venomous as the critic pleases, short of libel; what he must not do is set forth so much in quotation that the value of the original work is lost through its being read elsewhere. Fair Use is like an easement or a right of way through private property for the public's benefit. In that sense it really is an extension of the public domain. As public interest in the arts increases, the doctrine of Fair Use must expand with it.

Manner of Infringement

The manner by which infringement is accomplished also involves the public domain. Dramatic works, for example, must not be performed in public without the copyright owner's consent. The rule for musical compositions is less rigid, since the rule for drama ,here applied, would prevent whistling a tune in public. Musical works must not be performed "for profit" without the copyright owner's consent. The term "for profit" in the Act includes music played by cafe orchestras[20] or piped into hotel rooms[21] but allows anyone to whistle his head off whether the tunes are copyrighted or everyone's property. This is another of those easements across copyrighted private property that add a little to the public domain.

The creative artist is the law's alchemist. He is protected only when he turns old things into new; from the baser metals he must produce gold, or at least brass or pewter of his own making. All else is in the public domain.

The Rest is Yours

Summing up, the public domain is what you do *not* own. Nobody can "steal" your idea, theme, plot, setting, stock characters and so forth because they are in no way yours. They belong to the public along with the great masterpieces of the past which were never copyrighted in the United States at all. In addition the public at large may reproduce your work verbatim if the later work was independently composed without access to your own. You may also be quoted without permission within the reasonable limits of Fair Use. The public domain is the supreme negative to plaintiffs in the majority of infringement suits.

A new sense of humility is scarcely the sole purpose of exploring the public domain. The lesson to be learned from it is caution; I mean caution in divulging things before the time is ripe, as well as caution is imputing piracy where none exists. And now the other side of the borderline must be explored, the smaller area which you own by virtue of creating it. Here there are rights and remedies, not negatives and cautions. Here you find armories, not public playgrounds. Face to face now with your true brain child—a new means of expressing the old thoughts, stories, sounds and images in the public domain, and nothing more—you must take into account his unexpectedly small size and fight all the more devilishly to protect him.

5. Arrant v. Georgia Casualty Co., 212 Ala. 309, 311 (1924)
6. Bachman v. Belasco, 224 Fed. 817 (1915)
7. Roe-Lawton v. Hal E. Roach Studios, 18 F.(2d) 126 (1927)
8. Shipman v. R.K.O. Radio Pictures, Inc., 100 F.(2d) 533, 537 (1937)
9. Dymow v. Bolton, 11 F.(2d) 690, 691 (1926)
10. Wiren v. Shubert Theatre Corp., 5 F.Supp. 358 (1923)
11. Alexander v. Theatre Guild, Inc., 26 F.(2d) 741 (1927)
12. Lowenfels v. Nathan, 2 F.Supp. 73, 80 (1932)
13. 82 U. S. P. Q. 136, 208 P.(2d) 1 (1949)
14. 82 U. S. S. P. Q. 123, 208 P.(2d) 9 (1949)
15. Kelly v. Cinema Houses, Lt'd., Cacg. Cop. Cas. 362, 368 (1933)
16. Nichols v. Universal Pictures orp., 45 F.(2d) 119, 122 (1930)
17. Commonwealth v. Gordon, 66 D. & C. 101 (Pa. 1949)
18. Holmes v. Hurst, 174 U. S. 82, 86 (1898)
19. Sheldon v. Metro-Goldwyn Pictures Corporation, 81 F.(2d) 49, 54 (1936)
20. Herbert v. Shanley Co., 242 U. S. 591 (1917)

Chapter III

A REVIEW OF THE COPYRIGHT
ACT OF 1976

The copyright laws under which copyright protection was provided had been under fire not long after their enactment as The Copyright Act of March 4, 1909 "to promote the progress of science and the useful arts" pursuant to the United States Constitution.

So much of the advance in technology which has taken place since that time was of course not even a gleam in the eye of the laws' authors. Since 1909 there have emerged the silent and later, the sound, motion picture; radio and then television; even later cable and pay-television; computers and their accumulation and output of information; satellites and their potential for reaching and connecting everyone on earth; first sound recordings and now audio and video tape recordings; photocopying and microreprography; and automation in the composition and reproduction of printed matter. Nor does all of this exhaust the list, both presently existing and yet to come, which will bring about even further improvements and expansion in the dissemination of information and entertainment. Clearly, the 1909 copyright law could not and did not anticipate these developments and therefore could not cope with them.

Congressional efforts to revise the Copyright Law began as far back as 1924, but did not succeed in enacting a revised law until the passage of the Copyright Act of 1976 (Pub. L. No. 94-533, 90 Stat. 2541). This new statute specifies that, except for a number of exceptions, its provisions are effective as of January 1, 1978. Therefore, any cause of action in copyright arising before January 1977 is governed by the 1909 Act. Since there is a three-year statute of limitations in which such an action could be brought, the 1909 law can be applicable in such cases until 1981. Furthermore, the Transitional Section 103 of the new law also provides that no work that has fallen into the public domain before January 1, 1979 can be renewed under the new law. It is therefore important, for the next fifty years, to know whether publication occurred before January 1, 1978. If it does, the provisions of the old law will prevail.

Single System of Statutory Protection (Secs. 103 and 301)

Under the new law the old dual system of protecting works prior to publication under the common law and published works under federal statute has been abolished. A single system of statutory protection for all copyrightable works now governs. At the moment of its creation in a tangible form a copyright is created in a creative work. When writing an article, for example, a federally cognizable copyright exists the moment the writing instrument is lifted from the paper.

Section 301 of the copyright law applies to all works created after January 1, 1978 whether or not they are ever published or disseminated, so long as the works involved are "works of authorship that are fixed in a tangible medium of expression and come within the subject matter of copyright as specified by sections 102 and 103." All state laws on copyright, whether statutory or common law, are terminated on the effective date of the new law by reason of federal preemption. This means that after January 1, 1978 only the federal courts have jurisdiction over copyright matters. However, unless and until a work is "fixed" in a tangible medium of expression (either as a copy or a phonorecord) its common law copyright does not terminate, and its federal statutory copyright does not begin. Note the following three areas left unaffected by the preemption·

1. Works that do not come within the subject matter of federal copyright law;

2. Causes of action arising under state law before January 1, 1978;

3. Violations of rights not equivalent to any of the exclusive rights under copyright, such as unfair competition, deceptive trade practices and misappropriation.

Duration of Copyright (Secs. 302-305)

To the extent that common law copyright has not been preempted, it continues to exist in perpetuity. The new term of copyright applies to new works created after January 1, 1978 and to unpublished works already in existence on that date. If the work was created (first "fixed") on or after this date, the term of statutory copyright begins at the moment of creation and ends 50 years after the death of the author. In the case of joint authors, the 50-year period is based upon the life of the last surviving joint author. A special term is provided for anonymous and pseudonymous works as well as for works made for hire, even though such works were created on or after January 1, 1978. The new term is seventy-five years from the date of publication or one hundred years from the time of creation, whichever period expires earlier.

Unpublished works already in existence on January 1, 1978, which are not presently protected by statutory copyright and which have not yet gone into the public domain, are given the same Federal copyright protection prescribed for new works. Copyrights in older works of this kind, however, are provided special termination dates. Such protection will not expire prior to December 31, 2002, and if the work is published prior to that date, then protection will not expire prior to December 31, 2027.

For works already under statutory protection the new law retains the present term of copyright of twenty-eight years from first publication (or from registration in some cases), plus a renewal term except that the term of the renewal period is extended from 28 years to 47 years. This means that the total duration of statutory protection of such works is extended from 56 years after copyright was first secured to 75 years after such date.

Termination of Transfers

The transfer termination provisions of the new law are designed to benefit new authors. Under the old law, after the first term of twenty-eight years, the renewal copyright reverted in certain situations to the author or other specified beneficiaries. The new law drops the renewal feature except for works already in their first term of statutory protection on January 1, 1978. Instead, for transfer of rights made by an author or certain of the author's heirs after its effect date, the new law generally permits the author or certain of his heirs to terminate transfer after 35 years merely by serving written notice on the transferee within specified time limits. Such a termination of the grant may be effected notwithstanding any agreement to the contrary.

A similar right of termination is provided for works currently under statutory protection, but only with respect to transfers covering those years which extend the present maximum term of the copyright from 56 to 75 years. Within certain time limits, an author or specified heirs of the author are generally entitled to file notice terminating the author's transfers covering any part of the usual 19 years that have now been added to the end of the second term of copyright in a work already under protection when the new law comes into effect.

Works Protected (Secs. 102-103)

Section 102(a) of the Act provides that copyright protection subsists in "original works of authorship fixed in any tangible medium of expression, now known or later developed, from which they can be perceived, reproduced, or otherwise communicated, either directly or with the aid of the machine or device." The phrase in the old law, "writings of an author," has been replaced by "original works of authorship." The new law thereby avoids problems of interpretation of what "writing" means. But what constitutes an "original work of authorship," has not been changed. The description includes the following 7 categories:

1. literary works
2. musical works, including accompanying words
3. dramatic works, including any accompanying music
4. pantomines and choreographic works
5. pictorial, graphic and sculptoral works

6. motion pictures and other audio-visual works
7. sound records

Like the old law, in no case will copyright protection for an original work of authorship extend to an idea, procedure, process, system, method of operation, concept, principle or discovery, regardless of the form in which it is described, explained, illustrated or embodied in such work.

Also unchanged under the new law: "The copyright in a compilation or derivative work extends only to the material contributed by the author of such work, as distinguished from the pre-existing material employed in the work..." Copyright in new versions therefore extends only to the new material in the work. Also the new material cannot have any effect upon the nature of any copyright protection that may exist in the original work itself.

Provisions regarding "national origin" extend statutory protection in the law to unpublished works "without regard to the nationality or domicile of the author." Published works of foreign nations are eligible for United States copyright protection on the date of first publication if:

1. One of the authors is a national or domiciliary of the United States or a national or domiciliary of a foreign nation that is a party to a copyright treaty to which the United States is a party; or

2. The work is first published in the United States, or in a foreign country that is a party to the Universal Copyright Convention; or

3. The work is published by the United Nations or any of its specialized agencies, or by the Organization of American States; or

4. The work comes within the scope of a presidential proclamation.

The owner of the copyright is given the exclusive right to produce, to prepare derivative works, to distribute copies, and to perform publicly. The law explicitly gives the holder of the copyright the right to display the copyrighted work publicly in the case of literary, musical, dramatic, and choreographic works, pantomimes, and pictorial, graphic, or sculptoral works, including the individual images of a motion picture or other audio-visual work.

Government Publications (Sec. 106)

Works produced by the United States Government and its officers and employees, as part of their official duties are not subject to copyright protection. This places all such works whether published or unpublished, in the public domain.

Government officials and employees may, however, secure copyright in works they have written independently, outside their official duties, even though the subject matter involves their government work or professional field. A work privately copyrighted is protected regardless of subsequent publication by the government. Works generated by government research contracts, especially when commissioned by a government agency for its own use, can be denied copyright when it is in the public interest to do so.

Work for Hire (Sec. 201)

The new law incorporates the basic principle of the old law in the case of works made for hire. The employer is still considered the author of the work, and is regarded as the initial owner of copyright absent an agreement to the contrary. Any agreement under which the employee is to own rights must be in writing and signed by the parties. The impact of this provision is a copyright statute of frauds. No argument on behalf of the employee-author of an implied ownership of copyright will prevail.

The old law made no provisions for works made on commission or on special order by independent contractors. It was therefore within the discretion of the courts to interpret the rights in works created by an independent contractor. Under the new law, the copyright of a commissioned work belongs to the artist unless the work falls within the statutory definition of "a work made for hire."

Fair Use as a Limitation on Exclusive Rights (Sec. 107)

The new Act expressly codifies the judge-made doctrine of fair use as a limitation on the exclusive rights of copyright owners, and further indicates the factors to be considered in determining whether the use made is a "fair use":

1. The purpose and character of the use.
2. The nature of the copyrighted work.
3. The amount and substantiality of the portion used in relation to the copyrighted work as a whole.
4. The effect of the use upon the potential market for or value of the copyrighted work.

Multiple copies for classroom use are expressly mentioned as a use which may fall within the fair use defense just as are also mentioned criticism, comment, new reporting, scholarship, and research.

In addition, the House Report suggests certain guidelines with respect to photocopying by teachers. Under these, a teacher may make a single copy of a chapter of a book or of an article from a periodical or a newspaper, or a short story essay or a short poem, etc. Also, a teacher under such guidelines may make multiple copies for classroom use provided the following conditions are met:

1. Such copies are of an article of less than 2,500 words or of an excerpt from a work, which excerpt is not more than 1,000 words or 10 percent of the work, whichever is less.

2. Such copying is done on the initiative of the teacher at a time when it is unreasonable to expect a timely reply to a request for permission from the copyright owner.

3. Such copying is done for only one course, no more than one work is copied from a single author, no more than three authors are copied from a single collective work, and no more than nine instances of multiple copying occur during a single school term.

4. There is no copying of consummable work such as work books and standardized tests.

5. The same item is not reproduced from term to term.

6. No charge is made to the students beyond the actual cost of photocopying.

Library and Archives Photocopying (Sec. 108)

Separate from the defense of fair use, certain exemptions are conferred upon libraries and archives with respect to making or distributing single copies for noncommercial purposes. These institutions must be open to the public or to persons doing work in a single specialized field, and a notice of copyright must appear on the copies. Even if these conditions are complied with, photocopying by libraries and archives is exempt only in the following instances:

1. Reproduction of unpublished works for the purpose of preservation and security.

2. Reproduction for the purpose of replacement of damaged, deteriorating, lost, or stolen copies of additional unused copies cannot be obtained at a fair price.

3. Reproduction for patrons who obtain no more than a single copy of no more than one article or a small part of a work, and such copy becomes the property of the patron for purposes of study or research, and a copyright warning is displayed.

4. Reproduction of an entire work if a copyrighted work cannot be obtained at a fair price, and if the copy becomes the property of the user for study and research and a copyright warning is displayed.

A purely commercial enterprise could not establish a collection of copyrighted works, call itself a library or archive, and engage in for-profit reproduction and distribution of photocopies.

Librarians are relieved from an obligation to supervise photocopying under certain conditions. A library or archives or its employees are exempted from liability for the unsupervised use of reproducing equipment located on its premises. This exemption applies only if a notice is prominently displayed near the equipment, to the effect, that the unauthorized making of a copy of a copyrighted work may be an infringement of the copyright law. This exemption applies *only* to the institutions and their employees. The individual user making such an unauthorized copy may be liable.

Single copies used in interlibrary loan arrangements are

subject to specified limitations. It is permissible to reproduce an article, a short work in a copyrighted collection, or an issue of a periodical for distribution through an interlibrary loan. The copy must become the property of the user, and cannot be lent out and later recirculated. The use of the reproduction is limited to private study, scholarship or research. The library or archive must prominently display a warning of copyright both at the places where the orders are accepted and on the order form itself. However, the Act disables members of a network or consortium from sharing resources through interlibrary loan transactions involving multiple photocopies.

Copyright Royalty Tribunal (Secs. 801-810)

The Act establishes a Copyright Royalty Tribunal which determines whether copyright royalty rates in connection with sound recordings of music, playings on jukeboxes and cable television are reasonable and, if not, it will make adjustments accordingly. Under certain circumstances, the Tribunal will determine the distribution of those statutory royalty fees deposited with the Register of Copyrights. Also created is a form of compulsory licensing for the use of music and graphic works by non-commercial broadcasters, with the terms and rates of the licenses also to be set ultimately by this Tribunal if the Copyright owners and public broadcasting entities do not reach voluntary agreement.

Sound Recordings and Recording Rights in Music (Sec. 102 et seq)

Under the old copyright law sound recording copyrights were not protected until the Sound Recording Amendment of 1971. This amendment marked the first recognition in federal copyright law of sound recordings as copyrightable works. The new law retains the added provisions and accords protection against unauthorized duplication. It also raises the statutory royalty of compulsory license from the previous rate of two cents to a rate of two and three-fourths cents or one half cent per minute of playing time, whichever amount is larger.

There is, however, no performance right for sound recordings as such.

Limitation on Public Performance Rights (Sec. 110)

The Act accords the copyright owner comprehensive rights, exclusive in nature, concerning public performance of their works. It removes the old law's general exemption regarding not "for profit" public performances of non-dramatic literary and musical works. But the following specific types of public performance activities are exempted:

1. Face-to-face teaching activities in nonprofit educational institutions.

2. Transmission of a work if a regular part of the systematic activities of a nonprofit educational institution (or governmental body), if such performance is of material assistance to the teaching content of the transmission, and the transmission is made primarily for reception in classrooms or similar places or for reception of disabled persons or to governmental employees as a part of their duties.

3. Performances in the course of religious services of nondramatic literary or musical works, or of dramatic-musical works of a religious nature.

4. Performances of nondramatic literary and musical works (other than public transmission thereof) if this is done without any direct or indirect commercial advantage and without payment or compensation to the performers, promoters or organizers, if, further, there is no direct or indirect admission charge, or if there is such a charge the proceeds after deducting costs are for educational, religious or charitable purposes (unless the copyright owner has objected in writing to such a performance.

5. Communication to the public of a transmission of a performance (i.e., a multiple performance) on a single receiving set unless a direct charge is made or the communication goes beyond the place where the receiving apparatus is located.

6. Performances of nondramatic musical works at nonprofit agricultural fairs.

7. Performances of nondramatic musical works by and at

vending establishments for the sole purpose of promoting sales of copies or phonorecords of a work.

8. Certain transmissions of performances designed for and primarily directed to handicapped persons.

Jukebox Royalty (Sec. 116)

The Act requires the operator of a coin-operated phono-record player to obtain a compulsory license to perform the copyrighted music publicly on the phonorecord player. The owner must file an application, affix the certificate to the machine, and pay an annual royalty fee of eight dollars per jukebox to the Register of Copyrights for later distribution by the Copyright Royal Tribunal to the copyright owners. if such performances are made available on a particular phonorecord player after July 1 of any year, the royalty fee deposited for the remainder of that year is four dollars.

Cable Television and Secondary Transmission (Sec. 111)

This section deals with the complex and very significant economic problem of "secondary transmission." For the most part, this Section is directed to the operation of cable television systems (CATV) and the terms and conditions of their liability for the retransmission of copyrighted works.

A compulsory license for cable systems is established. The Act provides that any secondary transmission made to the public by a cable system, of a primary transmission made by a broadcast station licensed by the FCC or by an appropriate governmental authority of Canada or Mexico, is subject to compulsory licensing. The CATV operators are required to identify and record, then deposit with the Register of Copyrights a semi-annual statement of account, and finally, to make royalty fee payments for the period covered by the statement of account. The compulsory license provision applies only to the broadcast of the signals comprising the secondary transmission which is permissible under the rules and regulations of the FCC. Royalty payments are computed on the basis of specified percentages of the gross receipts from cable subscribers during the period covered by the statement. For purposes of computing royalty payments, only receipts concerning the basic service of providing secondary transmissions of primary broadcast transmitters are to be considered. Other receipts from subscribers such as those for pay-cable services or installation charges, are not included in gross receipts.

Certain secondary transmissions receive general exemptions. The first of these applies to secondary transmissions consisting "entirely of the relaying, by the management of a hotel, apartment house, or similar establishment" of a transmission to the private lodgings of guests or residents and provided "no direct charge is made to see or hear the secondary transmission." This exemption is not applicable if the secondary transmission consists of anything other than the mere relay of ordinary broadcasts. The deletion of advertising, the addition of new commercials, or any other change in the signal relayed would subject the secondary transmitter to full liability. Furthermore, the term "private lodgings" is limited to rooms used as living quarters or for private parties, and does not include dining rooms, meeting halls, theaters, ballrooms, or similar places that are outside of the normal circle of a family and its social acquaintances.

There are three additional exemptions provided for secondary transmissions:

1. An instructional transmission is exempted whether "primary or secondary" so long as it falls within the scope of Section 110.

2. A carrier is exempt if it has "no direct or indirect control over the content or selection of the primary transmission or over the particular recipients of the secondary transmission. For this purpose, its activities must "consist solely of providing wires, cables, or other communications channels for the use of others."

3. The operations of non-profit "translators" or "boosters," which do nothing more than amplify broadcast signals and retransmit them to everyone in an area for free reception, would be exempt if there is no charge to the recipient "other than assessments necessary to defray the actual and reasonable

costs of maintaining and operating the secondary transmission service."

This last exemption, however, does not apply to a cable television system.

Copyright Notice (Secs. 401-406)

The content of the copyright notice remains unchanged from the old law, except that unlike the 1909 Act, the year of first publication must be included in the notice even for pictorial, graphic and sculptoral works, with certain stated exceptions.

The form of this notice shall consist of the copyright symbol, the year of first publication, and the name of the copyright proprietor. The copyright symbol may be » (the letter C in a circle) or the word "Copyright," or the abbreviations "Corp."; for sound recordings the symbol (p) (the letter P in a circle) must be used.

The year date may be omitted, but where a pictoral, graphic or sculptoral work, with accompanying text matter, if any, is reproduced in or on greeting cards, postcards, stationery, jewelry, dolls, toys or any useful articles.

In cases involving compilations, or derivative works incorporating previously published material, the year of first publication of the compilation or derivative work is sufficient.

It should be noted that the outright omission of a copyright notice does not automatically forfeit copyright protection and cast the work into the public domain. This represents not only a major change in the theoretical framework of American copyright law, but it also will undoubtedly have immediate practical consequences in a great many individual cases. Omission of notice, whether intentional or unintentional, does not invalidate the copyright if either of two conditions is met: (1) if "no more than a relatively small number" of copies or phonorecords have been publicly distributed without notice, or (2) if registration for the work has already been made, or is made within five years after the publication without notice, and a reasonable effort is made to add notice to copies or phonorecords publicly distributed in the

United States after the omission is discovered. Therefore, if notice is omitted from more than a "relatively small number" of copies or phonorecords, copyright is not lost immediately, but the work will go into the public domain if no effort is made to correct the error or if the work is not registered within five years.

Innocent infringement of a work without notice is a defense to an action for actual or statutory damages. The burden is on the innocent infringer to prove that he did not have actual notice of the copyright and that he was misled by the lack of notice in order for the defense to prove that he did not have actual notice of the copyright and that he was misled by the lack of notice in order for the defense to be effective.

When a notice of copyright is defective because the name or date has been incorrectly stated, the result, while fatal under the old law, is not so under the new law. The validity of ownership of the copyright is protected where the registration has been made in the name of the true owner or where "a document executed by the person named in the notice and showing the ownership of the copyright has been recorded" in spite of defective notice. Defects due to wrongly stated dates include antedated and postdated notice. When the year in the notice is earlier than the year of first publication, however, the statutory term is computed from the year given in the notice. This applies to anonymous works, pseudonymous works, and works made for hire. When the year in the notice is one more than the year of first publication, it is treated as if the notice had been omitted and is governed by Section 405 in the Act. When the name or date is omitted from the notice, Section 406(c) provides that the work is considered by statute to have been published without any notice.

Registration and Deposit (Secs. 407-412)

Registration and deposit are not a condition of copyright, and even the failure to comply with a demand by the Register of Copyrights to make such deposit will not result in the loss of copyright but only in the imposition of a fine. A fine up to $250 for each work, plus the total retail price of the copies demanded or the reasonable cost expended by the Library of Congress in acquiring them, if no retail price has been fixed, can be imposed.

As under the 1909 Act, registration is a condition precedent to the bringing of an infringement action. Furthermore, registration prior to infringement is a condition to the right to statutory damages and attorneys' fees in actions for infringement of unpublished works and also (if registration is not made within three months of publication) to the same remedies for infringement of published works.

Remedies

Remedies under the new Act are essentially the same as those under the 1919 Act, except that the Act now makes explicit that the plaintiff is entitled to both actual damages and *additional* profits made by the defendant from the infringement. Also, statutory damages are an alternative to such actual damages and profits, and the plaintiff has the election whether he will take statutory damages or actual damages plus profits.

The computation of statutory damages has been altered. The minimum remains $250, but the maximum is changed from $5,000 to $10,000. There is under the new Act a statutory damage limitation of $50,000 even for willful infringement.

Finally, the awarding of costs to the prevailing party is discretionary with the court as is the awarding of attorneys' fees (both under the 1909 Act and the new Act).

Indivisibility of Copyright (Sect. 201(d)(2))

Since the old law spoke of a single "copyright" to which the author of a work was entitled, and referred to in the singular to "the copyright proprietor," it was inferred that the bundle of rights which accrue to a copyright owner were "indivisible," that is, incapable of assignment in parts. This concept of "indivisibility" if literally followed, rendered it impossible to assign anything less than the totality of rights commanded by copyright. Therefore, any grant of rights less than the entire copyright was regarded as merely a license, and not an assignment of ownership.

The new Act abolishes the "doctrines of indivisibility" and clearly states that "any of the exclusive rights comprised in a copyright, including any subdivision of any rights specified by Section 106, may be transferred... and owned separately. The owner of any particular exclusive right is entitled, to the extent of that right, to all of the protection and remedies accorded to the copyright owner under this title." This means that infringement takes place when any one of the rights is violated. There can no longer be any question about an author's right to divide up a copyright in the most remunerative way, and to retain for future bargaining those portions that he does not wish to include in the transfer.

Manufacturing Clause (Secs. 601-603)

On July 1, 1982, after 92 years as a form of trade protection for United States printing industries and American labor, the manufacturing clause will cease to be part of the copyright statute. During the interim period, the manufacturing clause will be substantially liberalized. The new law equates manufacture in Canada with manufacture in the United States. The requirement of manufacture in the United States or Canada is satisfied if the setting of type or the making of the plates has been performed in either of the two countries. Furthermore, this requirement for manufacture in the United States or Canada will apply only to works consisting principally of nondramatic literary material in English. Even where the work as a whole comes within the manufacturing requirement, those parts of it not subject to the clause (illustrations, foreign-language text, etc.) can be manufactured abroad. The requirement will apply only to works by American authors and will not apply where the author's permanent residence is outside the United States or where the individual author independently arranges for first publication outside the United States through a foreign publisher. Noncompliance does not invalidate the copyright, but may constitute a defense in an infringement action.

Chapter IV

THE PATENT APPLICATION

History of Patent Law

Patent laws were enacted as early as 1790 in the United States. Congress enacted these laws pursuant to authority derived from the Constitution. Since the granting of patents is governed by federal laws, the separate states have no power to determine whether a patent will be issued. If you have invented something which is patentable, you will acquire the same rights and be subject to the same duties, whether your brainchild was conceived in Brooklyn or in Boise. The laws of the United States will determine your right to a patent and once this right has been acquired, no state can limit it except in the exercise of its "police powers." Chapter IX dicusses state rights with regard to patents.

The original laws of 1790 were subsequently revised a number of times. In 1925 the Patent Office was transferred from the Department of the Interior to the Department of Commerce under whose jurisdiction it is today. The office is located in Washington, D. C.

The Patent office is charged with the duty of administering the laws relative to the granting of patents. It determines who is entitled to a patent and issues it to the deserving applicant. It publishes and keeps extensive records of all the United States patents granted since 1836. Its library contains more than 40,000 bound volumes of scientific periodicals and over 35,000 volumes of technical books. A Commissioner of Patents, appointed by the President of the United States, is the head of the office and he exercises a general supervisory power over the entire work of the Patent Office.

Purpose

Patent laws serve a dual purpose in this country. They are designed to protect the inventor or discoverer "of any new and useful art, machine, article of manufacture, composition of matter, or any new and useful improvement thereof." This result is accomplished by issuing "letters patent" to the inventor. This patent is a grant of certain rights and privileges made by the government to an inventor in return for which he must disclose his invention to the public. The inventor is granted a "monopoly" for a specific term of years during which time he has the right to exclude all the world from making, using or selling the invention without his authority.

By assuring the inventor that his rights will be adequately safeguarded for the period of seventeen years (less in the case of design patents), the second purpose of the patent statutes is fulfilled; that is "to promote the progress of science and useful arts by securing for limited times to . . . inventors the exclusive right to their respective . . . discoveries."[1]

In simple terms this means that if you have invented something new and useful, the government will grant to you a limited monopoly in your invention provided you disclose it to the public. Your rights are protected for seventeen years during which period you are free to do as you please with your invention or discovery. You may do nothing if you so desire, although this would scarcely be profitable. Or you may assign or sell or license some or all of your patent rights in return for royalties. After seventeen years, however, your rights expire and the public may use and practice your invention without obligation to you. In this manner, the patent system encourages the development of industry and science while assuring private citizens that their time and energy are not exploited without compensation. Inequities have occasionally arisen, of course, but the primary objective has been accomplished.

It may be well at this time to dispel several common

misconceptions with regard to patents, by stating the following "truths."

1. The issuance of a patent is no guarantee of commercial success or economic value of the invention or discovery. The patent office concerns itself only with the question of patentability.

2. Contrary to the wording of the statute and popular belief, the granting of a patent does NOT automatically include the right to manufacture and sell the invention. Although patentable, an invention may "infringe" some prior patent, thus subjecting the patentee (and the manufacturer) to a law suit for damages. The right that the patentee acquires is negative rather than positive. He can exclude others from making, using or selling his invention, although he may or may not acquire the unlimited right to these things himself.

3. A "patentability search" by a patent attorney is no guarantee that the invention is patentable.

4. A grant by the Patent Office is no guarantee that the patent does not infringe some prior patent or that it may not subsequently be declared invalid in a legal controversy. It does, however, bestow all rights and privileges on the inventor until the question of validity is raised.

5. The word "Reg. U. S. Pat. Office" denotes registration of a trademark and not that some article has been patented.

6. The words "Patent Pending" and "Patent Applied For" have no legal meaning. The word "Patent" followed by a number is the official way of indicating that a patent has been issued. The former terms are frequently used to inform the public that an application for a patent is pending in the Patent Office. They are also used for the purpose of attempting to scare off competitors.

7. The inventor or discoverer has a common law right today to enjoy the benefits of his invention, exclusive of the rights conferred by statutory provisions. He may keep his invention a secret. He need not apply for a patent.

However, once the general public learns of his invention, his protection is at an end. If he has not secured a patent under the patent laws, he may find that some more enterprising citizen has acquired superior rights. An inventor should not rely on his limited common law protection but should apply for a patent as soon as possible.

8. The inventor may apply for and prosecute his own patent application. The law has no specific requirement that he be represented by an agent or attorney. The Patent Office does suggest, however, that he retain legal counsel. Patent practice is highly specialized and errors in prosecuting a case may prove fatal. The application must be carefully drafted. For these reasons, the advice of the Patent Office should be taken. An attorney should certainly be consulted before the inventor signs any licensing, royalty or similar agreement. It may save him much grief and many dollars.

With these few admonitions in mind we may now turn to an examination of patent law and procedure.

What is Patentable

An invention or discovery which is both new and useful is patentable. The inventor need not have understood the scientific theory underlying his invention in order to qualify for the patent. And the fact that he stumbled upon his discovery will not operate to bar him from obtaining a patent. Ingenuity and originality are the determining factors. If an inventor's efforts resulted merely in some modification or improvement of an already existing invention or process, he would probably be denied a patent. The reason for these restrictions is fairly obvious. The government, when it issues a patent, is seeking to encourage and to reward inventors. If every minor change in the "prior art" were to merit a patent, the monopoly granted would be of little value to the inventor. Manufacturers would be reluctant to invest in new inventions for fear of being constantly involved in law suits. Thus, as science and art progress, it becomes increasingly difficult to invent or discover something which will ultimately meet the test of patentability.

The Statutory Provision

The Patent Laws expressly state which inventions are patentable. The applicable provision reads as follows.

"Any person who has invented or discovered any new and useful art, machine, manufacture, or composition of matter, or any new and useful improvements thereof. . . not known or used by others in this country before his invention or discovery thereof, and not patented or described in any printed publication in this or any foreign country, before his invention or discovery there, or more than one year prior to his application, and not in public use or on sale in this country for more than one year prior to his application, unless the same is proved to have been abandoned may upon payment of the fees required by law, and other due proceeding had, obtain a patent therefor."

It is obvious that this section of the law is complex and must be discussed in detail in order to be understood. If we divide the provision into three broad subdivisions, we may obtain some measure of clarity. Let us say that for an invention to be patentable it must meet the following primary requirements:

(A) It must be one of the types mentioned: either an art; or a machine; or an article of manufacture, or a composition of matter.

(B) It must meet the requirements of novelty and usefulness.

(C) The patent application must have been filed within the period prescribed by law where there has been public use, or sale, or publication or patenting subsequent to the inventor's date of invention but prior to his application for a patent.

An examination of each of these subdivisions follows:

(A) The terms "machine," "manufacture," "composition of matter" are self-explanatory. In patent law the word "art" usually refers to the process or method used to produce something, rather than to the thing or the actual result. Therefore, the means which produces a certain result may properly be the subject of a valid patent, as well as the result itself.

Although this section expressly provides that any "new and useful improvement" of an art, machine, etc., is patentable, the courts have generally denied the validity of improvement patents for the reasons set forth at the beginning of this chapter. Several types of improvements which have been held to be non-patentable include:

1. Improvements which merely strengthen an already patented device.

2. Or enlarge or make smaller something already patented.

3. Or change its form.

4. Or change the location of its parts; or reverse such parts.

5. Or make some change in degree.

6. Or substitute new parts for old parts without changing the results achieved.

Other types of inventions or discoveries have also been denied a patent, as for example the following:

Putting an old process or machine or composition of matter to a "New Use" is generally not patentable. Thus a patent was denied for a bicycle tire, where it was shown that automobile tires had already been patented.[2] And a patent was refused on street shoes using a wedge type sole, where it was shown that wedges on house slippers had already been patended.[3]

Ideas or abstract principles are not patentable as such. But the result accomplished by the application of an idea is patentable. A patent will not be issued for the discovery of a phenomenon of nature. A combination of individual elements which are old in the art may nevertheless be patentable, where these old elements when combined produce a new result or a distinctive device.

Although the popular types of patents are Mechanical Patents, Process and Composition Patents are also common. Design Patents differ in some respects from the types just mentioned.

Design Patents

A person who invents any original and ornamental design for an article of manufacture may be granted a design patent. Ordinary craftsmanship will not be rewarded. The inventor must show initiative and originality. Generally, the rules and regulations which apply to patents for inventions and discoveries also apply to patents for designs. There are, however, a few noteworthy differences.

Design patents are granted for a three and one half year term, a seven year term, or a fourteen year term. The period desired must be specified in the patent application. The patent fees will differ according to the term designated. On filing an application for a term of

    (a) Three and one half years, the fee is........$10.00
    (b) Seven years $15.00
    (c) Fourteen years $30.00

The measure of damages for infringement of a design patent also differs from the general rule in patent cases (see p. 35). The infringer is immediately liable in the amount of $250 and is further responsible for any profit he has made in excess of the sum of $250. (The provision as to triple damages, however, does not apply to design patents.)

(B) Assuming that the invention comes within the classifications set out in subdivision (A), the Patent Office Examiner will make a further study to see whether the invention is also new and useful. He will use these tests.

(1) If the invention was KNOWN to others in this country before the legal date of your INVENTION, then it is not new.

(2) If it was USED by others in this country before the legal date of your INVENTION, then it is not new.

(3) If it was PATENTED in this or in any foreign country before you INVENTED it, then it is not new.

(4) If it was disclosed in a PRINTED PUBLICATION

in this or in any foreign country before you INVENTED it, then it is not new.

For the purpose of this test, the controlling factor is the DATE ON WHICH YOU MADE YOUR INVENTION. It is for this reason that inventors are constantly cautioned to keep a complete and dated record of their inventions from the date of original conception to the date on which the patent finally issued.

In determining whether something is patentable, the Patent Office examiner will search the prior art to see if the invention has not been "anticipated."

Anticipation

If the subject matter which an applicant seeks to patent is known, or used or published prior to the date of his own invention, then any patent which he might receive would be invalid on the grounds of lack of novelty. The patent has been anticipated. Where two persons claim to have made the same invention. only one of them is legally entitled to the patent. That person is the first inventor. Thus if the Patent Office examiner finds that a patent had already been granted prior to the legal date of your invention, either by the United States or a foreign government, for the very thing which you now seek to patent, then your application will be denied. Your patent was anticipated and would be invalid if issued. The fact that you had no knowledge of the prior patent and that you made your invention independently is no defense.

If the subject matter of your patent has already been disclosed in a printed publication, either here or abroad, prior to the legal date of your invention, then your patent will not be granted. This rule applies even though you were never aware of the publication and even though the publication was not printed in this country. Any disclosure, whether in a scientific magazine, book, or thesis, is sufficient to constitute a printed publication. The description must, however, be complete with respect to the invention that it discloses, and a mere hint or suggestion may not amount to anticipation.

Where there is "public use" in this country, of the subject matter of your invention, and such use preceded the date of your invention, then your patent should be denied on the ground of lack of novelty. The fact that there is no prior patent in existence in this country does not change the rule. Public use or knowledge, however derived, is enough to constitute anticipation of your patent. But knowledge or use in a foreign country of an invention which is unpatented and unpublished will not prevent the issuance of a patent in the United States, provided the inventor states under oath in his application that he believes himself to be the original inventor. Public use must be distinguished from private or experimental use. Where an inventor merely tests his invention to see whether it works, such experimental use will not amount to public use or sale, provided the tests are primarily for the purpose of experiment and not for commercial exploitation of a completed invention. Experiments which have been abandoned without success do not constitute an anticipation.

(C) After your invention has met the requirements of subdivisions (A & B) (e.g.) you have invented a machine, not known or used by others in this country before the date of your invention; and not patented or described in any printed publication in this or in any foreign country prior to the date of your invention—you must still comply with the requirements of subdivision (C). If you fail to do so you will lose your rights to obtain a patent, even though you are otherwise fully qualified.

For this test, the controlling factor is the DATE ON WHICH YOU FILED YOUR APPLICATION FOR A PATENT. Under subdivision (B) we saw that public use, knowledge, publication or patenting **prior** to the DATE OF YOUR INVENTION would invalidate your patent on the grounds that it was not new. Under subdivision (C) we find that public use, knowledge, sale, patenting or publication **subsequent** to the DATE OF YOUR INVENTION may constitute a bar to your right to a patent. The reason in this case is not lack of novelty since the priority of your invention is not questioned. There is no doubt that your invention preceded such public use, sale, etc. Why then should your patent be refused? The theory behind the rule is that an inventor may succeed in unlawfully extending his seventeen year monopoly by permitting his invention to be used and sold publicly, while withholding his patent application for an additional number of years. To forestall this possibility, the law practically forces the inventor to file his patent application within one year of the date of his invention. He is not absolutely required to do so. However, failure to make such timely application may be fatal. For example:

1. A patent will not be issued to you on your invention if it has been patented in the United States or in a foreign country more than one year prior to the date of your application. This means that, even though you are admittedly the original inventor, you will lose your right to a patent, unless you file your application within one year from the date on which the patent was first granted.

2. A patent will not be issued to you on your invention if it has been described in any printed publication in this or in any foreign country more than one year prior to the date of your application. This simply means that, although you are unquestionably the original inventor, you will lose your right to a patent, unless you file your application within one year from the date of publication. This rule applies even though the disclosure or publication was made by you. Your own disclosure may be a bar unless you comply with the statute. In order to be absolutely safe, you should apply for your patent as soon as possible after you have invented anything; but in no event should you permit more than one year to elapse between these two dates.

3. A patent will not be issued to you on your invention if it has been in public use or on sale in the United States for more than one year prior to the date of your application.

This means that even though you are admittedly the original inventor, you will lose your right to a patent, unless you file your application within one year from the date on which there has been a public use or sale. Experimental use or secret use by the inventor does not come within the rule, since the inventor is not thereby seeking to extend his monopoly. However, he runs the risk of someone learning of his invention and acquiring superior rights. Therefore, if your invention has been reduced to practice, it is not advisable to delay filing your application. Experiments may be conducted while the application is pending.

An inventor may also lose his right to obtain a patent where he abandons his invention.

Abandonment

Abandonment can be proved against an inventor by showing that he has failed to reduce his invention to practice, or that he has permitted it to be used by the general public more than one year before he applied for a patent. An invention once abandoned is lost forever. However, an application for a patent may be abandoned and subsequently renewed with the approval of the Patent Office.

If your invention can successfully withstand the tests set out above in subdivisions A, B and C, then it is patentable.

Who May Obtain a Patent

If you have invented or discovered something which is patentable, you may obtain a patent in the United States regardless of your age or sex. The fact that you are not a citizen will not bar you. Employees of the Patent Office, however, are not permitted to obtain patents during the period of their employment. Any other government employee may receive a patent. The true inventor (or inventors) is the only person who may apply for a patent. He must sign the application and execute the oath.

Fiduciaries and Guardians

If the inventor has died before applying for a patent or after filing his application and before the patent has been granted, the right passes to his executor or administrator. They in turn hold this right in trust for the distributees of the deceased inventor. Where the inventor has become insane before a patent has been granted, his legally appointed guardian or representative may obtain the patent.

Joint Inventors

Where two or more persons have combined their talents to conceive and perfect an invention, they are bound to join in the application for the patent. This concept of joint inventors is narrowly construed by the courts. A financier or an advisor is not considered a co-inventor. Neither is an employer nor the person who subsequently manufactures the invention. Assignees, grantees and licensees are not joint inventors. Where an invention has been jointly conceived, all the inventors must apply for the patent. The application must be made jointly and each inventor must take the oath. A patent which has been issued to only one of two inventors is invalid. A patent which has been issued to co-inventors, while there was in truth but a single inventor, is also invalid. These restrictions are readily understandable. Joint owners have equal powers with regard to patent rights. Either one, without the consent of the other, may grant a license or otherwise act independently. Thus the law imposes safeguards.

ASSIGNEES

An inventor frequently assigns the whole or a part of his invention. He may be forced to do this for financial reasons. Not every inventor has the money or means with which to pursue his invention. He may find it necessary to assign his rights for the purpose of securing the facilities to build and perfect his invention. The assignment may be given before he files his patent application or subsequent thereto. The application must in either case be signed by the inventor. Where a part interest has been assigned, the patent will issue in the name of both the patentee and the assignee. Where the assignment was of the entire interest, the patent will generally be issued in the assignee's name.

It has been stated that only the true inventor may apply for a patent. While this may be necessary in order to comply with the procedural requirements of the Patent Office, it is no indication of who actually owns the patent rights. Who is legally entitled to use, sell license, assign or otherwise distribute patent rights? It may not be the true inventor. There are various factual possibilities which create a problem of conflicting rights and interests. For example:

1. Two persons have jointly conceived and developed an invention. What are their rights ith respect to each other and to third persons?

2. The inventor has assigned all or some part of his rights in his invention or in his patent. What rights does the assignee acquire by virtue of either of these assignments?

3. The owner of an invention on which a patent has been issued subsequently licenses another person to practice or use the invention. What may he expressly license by contract and which rights are implied in law?

4. An employee conceives and perfects his invention while so employed. The employer claims ownership rights in the invention. Who will prevail?

The factual possibilties are endless and could easily be the subject of a separate book. For this reason it would be unwise to attempt to set out any specific "rules of law." Each case must be decided on its individual facts. The author can only hope to make the reader aware of some of the factors which influence the courts in deciding who is the owner where conflicting interests are involved.

1. Joint Inventions

In addition to what has already been said in Chapter III, the following general rules should be remembered. Where there are joint inventors, either has the power to grant a license under the patent, thereby binding the other. It would further seem to be the law that neither co-inventor is liable to his partner for profits or royalties, in the absence of an express agreement. It becomes important, therefore, where several persons are working on the same invention, that they take legal steps to safeguard their individual rights, thus avoiding any future misunderstanding. An agreement among them at the outset may accomplish the purpose.

2. Assignor-Assignee

In the parlance of patent law, "assignment" may have several meanings. It may constitute a transfer of an undivided part of the inventor's entire interest. Or it may refer to a transfer of the entire interest in some invention, or a transfer of Patent Rights, or both. As previously indicated, the application for a patent must be in the inventor's name even though an assignment has been made. Assignments must be in writing and should be recorded immediately in the Patent Office. Failure to record may impair the assignee's rights. If the assignment has preceded the issuance of the patent, it must be recorded or else the patent will not be issued in the assignee's name. If you are the assignee of valuable rights in a patent and fail to record your agreement, a subsequent purchaser or mortgagee of the patent will acquire title free and clear of your interest provided he has no **actual** notice of your assignment. To forestall this possibility, you must record. All subsequent purchasers and lienors are then put on "constructive notice" of your prior interest, and you are completely protected. The assignment conveys an ownership right in the invention or the patent.

The assignee may thereafter exercise the rights and privileges which are consistent with his status as owner.

Licenses (Express licenses)

A license is a contract in which the owner of the patent

grants to another some rights in the patent. Unlike an assignee, the licensee does not acquire a full ownership interest. As licensee he may acquire authority to manufacture or to use the patented article. His use, without the license, would put him in jeopardy of a law suit.

If you own a patent you will probably wish to exploit its usefulness to your best advantage. You will be interested in making an agreement which will assure you the best financial returns. You are not bound, however, to use or manufacture your invention. The granting or withholding of a license is entirely within the patentee's discretion. The terms of the license will vary as in any contractual agreement. They will depend on the nature of the invention, its use, manufacturing problems, competition, public demand, economic factors and numerous other considerations. The owner of the patent must bargain away his property rights in return for royalties. His bargaining powers are determined by whether he is rich or poor, young or old, where he works, whom he knows, and so forth. The owner seeks to surrender as little as possible, while the licensee bids for the best arrangement he can buy. The owner may impose restrictions on the licensee. Pursuant to the agreement, he may limit the quality or quantity of the article to be manufactured or sold, or the time or place where it may be manufactured or sold. The courts interpret these licensing contracts in conformity with their express provisions. Implied and collateral powers will not generally be read into a license. Thus, a license to manufacture the patented article does not carry an implied right to sell what has been manufactured. Nor may a licensee use the patented device, if he has only been granted the privilege of selling it.

The owner of a patent should secure competent legal advice before entering into any agreement. The attorney recognizes factors unknown to a layman. It may be possible to effect substantial tax savings. Your patent rights, though intangible, are property, no less valuable than your home, your automobile or the securities you own. You should treat these rights with equal care.

Employer-Employee

Where the relationship of employer and employee exists, many factors are important in determining who owns the patent. Did the employee use his employer's tools and equipment? Was the work done on the employer's time? Who originally conceived the invention? Did the employer suggest the idea to the employee and was the latter expressly hired to perfect it? Was the employee hired "to invent" or was the invention something outside the scope of his regular labors? These are but a few of the questions that the courts must consider where litigation develops. Several general rules may be stated, but it should be remembered that even a slight variation in the factual pattern may lead to a different result.

The simplest case is where a person is employed for the express purpose of inventing something specific. If the employee's efforts are successful while so employed, then the invention or discovery belongs to the employer. A problem arises, however, where the employment is general rather than coupled with the duty to invent.

If the employee makes his invention or discovery while working in a factory of his employer and with the use of his tools and facilities and on the company's time, what will be the result? The employee probably retains the ownership right to the patent and its use, but the employer acquires a shopright.

Shopright

As the word itself indicates, a shopright will arise where an employee makes an invention in his employer's shop, using the latter's equipment. The employer receives the right to use the invention without paying any royalty to the employee-inventor. This right is in the nature of an implied license and will generally be limited in scope. It is personal to the employer and may not be assigned. It is what the law reserves to the employer, because of the nature of the circumstances. The shopright is co-extensive with the life of the patent and is not extinguished by any grant, assignment or license which the patentee may subsequently make.

Where an employer hires an employee to experiment on and to improve the employer's existing invention, then the results of the employee's work will probably belong to his employer.

It is now common for employers to require employees to sign written stipulations to the effect that any inventions made during the period of employment must be assigned to the employer. The courts have upheld the validity of these agreements provided they are not too broad in scope. The nature of the employment may well determine the permissable breadth and scope of these contracts.

The Patent Petition

This is the formal request for a patent grant. It is directed to the Commissioner of Patents and includes the name and address of the petitioner.

The Oath

The inventor must swear that to his best knowledge, he is the original or first inventor of the article which he seeks to have patented. He must further specifically allege under oath that he does not believe that the invention was ever previously known or used. The application should never be signed or sworn to in blank. It should be closely inspected by the applicant before he affixes his signature.

Specification

The invention must be described in detail in this part of the application. The description must be so clear that any person who is skilled in that particular field could construct or use the article after reading the specification. The inventor must explain the principle of his invention and the manner in which it is to be used. In short, the specification must be so fully detailed as to give other persons a complete understanding of the invention or discovery, where such persons are likewise skilled in the art to which the invention refers.

The Claims

A claim is an example or some embodiment of what the specification reveals. The claims define the scope of the discovery or invention and determine the patentee's rights. They enable the patent examiner to determine what is new and useful and not merely part of the prior art. Claims which are too broad may be disallowed by the examiner, but those which are too specific may result in unexpected restrictions on the inventor's monopoly. There is no legal limit to the number of claims which the inventor may specify. He is entitled to twenty claims as part of his original patent fee. For each additional claim over twenty, he is charged $1. Every claim set forth is separate and distinct and entitles the inventor to an additional lawful monopoly.

The advice and assistance of an experienced patent draftsman should be sought to help prepare the claims. Faulty drafting may result in irreparable harm to the applicant's cause. If an inventor fails to claim what he has invented, such matter becomes part of the public domain. Particular care must be exercised in claiming what has been disclosed in the specification. It cannot be too strongly emphasized that expert advice should be solicited.

Drawings

Drawings must be furnished wherever practicable. The Rules of Practice of the Patent Office set out detailed regulations in the interest of clarity and uniformity as to the use of drawing paper, ink, sheet size, margins, scale, reference, characters, symbols and legends. Applicants are advised to employ competent draftsmen to make their drawings. A model or specimen may be requested by the patent office in its discretion, but it is not otherwise required.

Fees

Upon filing an application for a patent which has twenty claims or less, the inventor is charged $30. When a patent is issued, he pays a final fee of $30 plus an additional $1 for each claim in excess of twenty. For complete details as to fees see pages 70-71. The final fee must be paid before the patent will be issued and not later than six months after the applicant receives notice that his application has been approved. A patent is generally issued within three months from the date on which final fees have been paid.

Issuing the Patent

Your application has been filed and you have paid the fee required by law. An examination of the invention will now be made by an examiner in the Patent Office. The purpose of this examination is to determine whether your invention or discovery is new, useful and important enough to warrant the granting of a patent.

The Patent Office

The Patent Office library has compiled a complete record of the prior art. Aside from copies of all the United States patents issued since 1836, which are available to the public, the examiner has at his disposal over six million copies of foreign patents, besides foreign and American publications. His search is far more exhaustive than that of a patent attorney. Pending applications, which are carefully secreted from public inspection, are within the scope of the patent examiner's search.

Patents are divided into classes in the office files in order to expedite the search. The application is referred to the examiner in charge of that class or subdivision to which it pertains. He then inspects the application as to form and substance. It must initially comply with the formal requirements set forth in the Patent Laws and

Rules of Practice of the United States Patent Office. Secondly, it must disclose something which is not prior art, but is new and useful.

If the application is found proper as to the formal requirements, the decision of the examiner will then concern the merits of the petition. He will decide whether the invention is patentable. The tests for patentability have already been discussed in Chapter II.

If the application is rejected, the applicant must be notified of the reasons therefor. He is then entitled to a Re-examination of his application after receiving notice of rejection. He may request reconsideration without altering his original claims or specifications, by arguing that the examiner has erred in his initial determination. Or he may amend his application and show how his amendment avoids the grounds for rejection. The Patent Office Rules which govern the making of amendments are too complex and detailed to be discussed here. It is sufficient for our immediate purpose to know that by permitting the liberal use of amendments, the Patent Office assures each applicant complete and just consideration before it takes any final action. An applicant must generally respond within six months to any action taken by the examiner. Failure to prosecute your case within this period (or a lesser time if set by the Patent Office) will result in your application being deemed abandoned.

Some applications may result in the declaration of an "interference" by the Patent Office.

Interferences

Where an inventor applies for a patent which claims the same patentable invention as another pending application or patent, the Commissioner of Patents may order a proceeding to determine the question of priority of invention. This is known as an "Interference." A Board consisting of three special interference examiners conducts the hearing and makes a determination as to who is entitled to the patent. In an Interference the burden of proving priority of invention rests on the "junior party." That means that the person who has filed his application first (senior party) is presumed to have made his invention before the party who filed his application later (junior party). The latter must therefore prove that although he filed last, he invented first. He must further prove that he was acting diligently from the date of his invention down to the date that he filed his application. This once again illustrates the impor-importance of filing a patent application as soon as possible after the date of invention. In an Interference, proof that you invented first is not conclusive of your right to a patent unless you can also show that you did not unreasonably delay in filing your patent application. The procedure and the rules of evidence which govern Interferences are beyond the scope of this brief monograph. They may be found in the Rules of Practice of the United States Patent Office. It should be indicated, however, that the Commissioner has the authority to issue a patent to the party whom the Board of Interference Examiners adjudges to be the prior inventor. The decision of this Board is subject to court review.

The Patent

If the examiner shall finally decide that the application warrants the issuance of a patent, he will notify the applicant and his attorney. Final fees must be paid or else the application may become forfeited. Assignments should be recorded before final fees are paid, otherwise the patent will be issued to the inventor rather than to the assignee. The patent will bear the seal of the Patent Office and be issued in the name of the United States and mailed to the patentee or his attorney. The monopoly granted may not be renewed at the expiration of its term. At that time it becomes part of the public domain.

Chapter V

APPEAL PROCEDURE AND INFRINGEMENT

An applicant is entitled to appeal from the primary examiner's decision which rejects his claims. His appeal must be made to an administrative group known as the Board of Appeals.

Board of Appeals

This Board is empowered to review the decision of the examiner and to reverse or modify it where the applicant can show sufficient reasons to warrant such action. The Board consists of the following persons: The Commissioner of Patents; the First Assistant Commissioner; Assistant Commissioners; Examiners in Chief. Appeals are generally heard by at least three members who have been designated by the Commissioner.

Judicial Review

A ruling by the Board of Appeals exhausts the applicant's administrative remedies where a rehearing or re-argument is also denied. He must now resort to the courts for further consideration. If the decision of the Board does not satisfy the applicant he is entitled to prosecute his case in one of two ways.

1. By appealing the decision to the United States Court of Customs and Patent Appeals; or

2. By bringing a bill in equity in the district court of the United States to obtain his patent.

If he chooses to go before the Court of Customs and Patent Appeals, he waives his right to the other remedy. There are several important differences betwen these two remedies. The decision of the Court of Customs and Patent Appeals is final. The suit in equity, however, may be carried through the federal Court of Appeals to the Supreme Court of the United States. A bill in equity is in the nature of an "independent action" to obtain a patent and the petitioner is permitted to introduce new evidence which is not on record in the Patent Office proceedings. In his appeal to the Court of Customs and Patent Appeals, however, he is bound by the record compiled below, and may not introduce any further evidence to support his case.

In the final analysis, the applicant will choose the remedy he can best afford. His resources may be such that he will be unable to pursue his rights beyond the primary examiner's decision. Appeal litigation is expensive.

Infringement

You have invented something new and useful and have secured a patent. You learn that the EZ company subsequently manufactures your invention without ever having received any license or assignment from you. They are infringing your patent rights.

Your next door neighbor starts using an exact copy of your invention without your permission a few weeks after you have been issued a patent. He is an infringer.

You have patented your invention and you read in the newspaper one day that John Doe, who lives in a city 2000 miles from your town, has invented an identical or similar device, that he has licensed the EZ company to manufacture it and has agreed to permit its sale through the XY agency. Neither Doe nor the EZ company nor the agency ever heard of your invention. All believe Doe to be the inventor of a new and original device. They may all be guilty of infringing your patent. Should you choose to enforce your legal rights, the fact that their infringement was in ignorance of the true facts and unintentional will not constitute a defense. The court will concern itself only with the question of whether you have been damaged by their acts.

Assume, however, that you sell your invention to your next door neighbor or that you permit him to build and use your invention BEFORE you apply for a patent. He will not be liable to you as an infringer. He may continue to use or sell your invention even after your patent application is approved.

Infringement may, therefore, be defined as the nonsanctioned manufacture, use, making or sale of an invention for which a valid patent has been issued. Appropriating the essential features of a patented invention constitutes an infringement. A determining factor will generally be whether the infringing device uses substantially the same means to produce a result identical to that of the prior patent. The fact that the "form" of the infringing device is different will not avoid the penalty where the principle and the results are similar or alike. The same rule applies where the only difference is in the use of some "equivalent" which achieves no new result.

Defenses

In an infringement suit, the defendant may put in issue the validity of the patent purportedly infringed. This means that if A sues B for infringing his patent, B may defend by showing that A's patent is invalid and therefore cannot be infringed. The defendant, however, bears the burden of proving his defense of invalidity. He can accomplish this by proving on trial any one or more of the following matters:

1. That the invention had already been patented before the plaintiff supposedly made his own invention.

2. Or that it had been described in a printed publication prior to the time the plaintiff allegedly made his invention.

3. Or that it had been patented or described in a printed publication prior to the date on which the plaintiff filed his application for a patent AND such filing date was more than one year after the date of patenting or publication.

4. Or that it had been on sale, or used by the public in this country prior to the date on which the plaintiff filed his application for a patent AND such filing date was more than one year after the date of such public use or sale.

5. Or that the plaintiff was not the original inventor of the thing patented.

6. Or that the plaintiff had abandoned his invention to the public.

The defendant must produce specific and detailed information (names, dates, addresses, etc.) to support his defense or else he will fail to sustain his burden of proof.

Liability for Infringement

The suit for infringement must be commenced within six years from the date of the alleged injury. It should be started as soon as practicable. The claimant is entitled to recover damages if he can prove his case and the courts are also empowered to grant injunctive relief where proper. A unique provision in the patent laws permits the court to increase any verdict which may have been rendered against an infringer up to three times its original amount.

Marking

If you have received a patent on your invention and wish to license it for manufacture or sale, you must be sure that the article is properly marked. This is done in order to notify the public that the article is patented. Failure to mark may defeat your legal right to sue for damages for infringement. By fixing the word "Patent" together with its number on the invention, you are deemed to have put the world on notice as to your prior rights. Anyone who subsequently makes, uses or sells the article, without your approval is liable to you in damages. If it is impossible to mark the article itself, then the package containing it or a label should be marked as indicated. Falsely labeling an unpatented article with the word "Patent" is an offense punishable by a heavy fine. The phrases "Patent applied for" and "Patent pending" have no legal meaning.

Chapter VI

PATENT STRATEGIES

The preceding chapters have been concerned primarily with the rules and with some procedural provisions which affect the prospective patentee. It must have been apparent to the reader, however, that strategies are exceedingly important. Doing the right thing at the proper time is probably more essential in this field of law than in any other. The inventor who fails to realize this will soon come to grief. In no other field of law is detail so important or punctuality so vital. The reasons for these stringent requirements are worthy of review.

Preliminary Protection

We have seen that an inventor is given some measure of protection other than the rights he acquires under the patent laws. As a general rule, however, he should not rely on this limited "common law" protection. An inventor has no right to exclude others from making, using or selling his invention until he has secured a patent. By keeping his idea a secret he runs the risk of someone getting superior rights to the same invention. Therefore, an inventor, should take advantage of the protection expressly granted to him by the Patent Laws of the United States. The first step in this process is to prepare a disclosure at the earliest possible time.

The Disclosure

At some time during the period that his application is pending and before the patent office will be willing to grant a patent, the inventor may be required to prove that he is the original or first person to have conceived the thing which he seeks to have patented. In order to meet this challenge he must be able to present adequate evidence of prior conception. An inventor should, therefore, make a written record of his invention as soon as is feasable. This record should include all his notes, sketches, and descriptions, no matter how incomplete or crude. These papers should be DATED and WITNESSED by a person who can be trusted. This record may be introduced as evidence of the date on which the invention was first conceived. Some inventors accomplish the same result by enclosing the above mentioned papers in a self addressed envelope which is then sent to the addressee by registered mail. The envelope remains sealed until proof of conception is requird. This method eliminates the necessity of finding someone who can be trusted to witness the primary disclosure.

Having disclosed this preliminary record, the inventor should immediately proceed to apply for his patent. The fact that the invention has not as yet been perfected or reduced to practice will not bar his application. He may continue to work on his invention after the application has been filed.

An inventor may prepare and prosecute his own application for a patent. The Patent Office recommends however, that he retain competent legal advice. This suggestion, if taken, may enable an inventor to avoid needless expense and effort. A registered patent attorney will conduct his own preliminary patentability search before permitting his client to invest in a formal application on an invention which may subsequently prove unpatentable.

Preliminary Patentability Search

This is a search made by a patent attorney, who examines the records in the Patent Office and renders his opinion as to whether the invention is patentable. He performs his search before he permits his client to file the formal application for a patent. If, in his opinion, the disclosure made to him shows nothing patentable, he will advise against any further steps by the inventor. If his examination of the prior art leads him to conclude that the invention is patentable, then he will so advise his client. The search will subsequently be of definite value to the draftsman who must determine how broad to draft the patent claims, in the application. It must be emphasized, however, that the patent attorney is rendering at best only his opinion. His search is limited. He is not permitted to examine all the records in the Patent Office. Pending applications are kept secret and are not available for inspection to the public. Many foreign patents and publications may not be at his disposal. In spite of these limitations, however, his opinion as to patentability should be a valuable guide for the inventor. If his search is favorable, a formal patent application should immediately be prepared.

The Patent Application

The patent application should be filed as soon as possible. In no event, however, should it be filed later than one year after the date of conception. A longer delay may result in an automatic forfeiture of the inventor's right to a patent. There are several tactical reasons why an early filing is advised.

1. The official application constitutes a "constructive reduction to practice" of the invention. Once it is filed, no question may be raised as to whether the inventor has acted with reasonable diligence in perfecting his invention.

2. A party who can show a prior filing date is at a definite advantage in an interference proceeding since the burden of proof falls on the party who has filed last to prove that he was the first inventor.

3. Since an inventor may sell his invention for commercial usage BEFORE he has obtained a patent, he must be certain to file his application no later than one year after such public sale or use. No patent will be issued for an invention which has been on public sale or in use in the United States earlier than one year before the date of filing of the patent application.

4. The same time limitations apply where an inven-

tion is described in a printed publication anywhere in the world. The inventor must file his patent application within one year of the date of publication to prevent a forfeiture of his right to the patent.

5. Even if there has been no prior public use or sale, it is advisable to file the application immediately after conceiving or disclosing the invention. This avoids the possibility of an inventor of the same or a similar thing from showing a prior filing date thus shifting the burden to you to prove priority of conception.

We know that the patent application consists of the petition, oath, specification, claims, drawings and sketches. The most important single part from a tactical viewpoint is "The Claims." Although patents are generally issued on the merits of the invention, drafting imperfections may unwittingly limit the scope of the grant. It is for this reason that the assistance of an expert should be procured.

The Claims

The claims measure, control and limit the scope of the patent. The patentee is bound by the language which he uses. If his application discloses something patentable which he fails to claim, he is held to have dedicated it to the public. An inventor cannot subsequently claim what he has once dedicated to the public, even though he was the first or original inventor.

The very words and phrases used in setting forth patent claims are vitally important. Many terms commonly used have been interpreted by the courts. They have acquired special meanings with regard to patent law, separate and apart from their everyday meanings. A patent attorney is aware of these limitations. He knows that words such as "several," "consists of," "comprises," "integral," "adjacent," "inclined," etc., to suggest but a few, have been judicially construed and he uses them in the light of his special knowledge. The necessity for ingenuity and skill in the preparation and prosecution of patent claims cannot be too greatly emphasized.

Drawing and Models

When the date of the invention must be proved, the drawings or a model of what has been invented are the primary factors. Mere proof of the date on which the invention was conceived will not be accepted as conclusive evidence of the true date of invention. For this reason it is wise to date and disclose all drawings and sketches and to keep them in a safe place.

Patent Agreements

An inventor may assign, sell or license his patent rights. If he does, he should have his attorney prepare a detailed, written contract. Little, if anything should be left unmentioned. The interpretation of an incomplete agreement by a court may differ materially from that which either of the parties contemplated. To forestall this possibility, the contracting parties should expressly state their rights and duties.

A licensing agreement to manufacture, for example, should contain provisions other than the usual limitations as to duration, royalties, quality and quantity. Some of the following rights and duties should be specifically covered in the contract:

1. Territorial restrictions, if any.
2. Whether the licensee may sublicense or assign.
3. Whether the licensor is obligated to protect the licensee against infringers. In the absence of an express agreement to this effect, the licensor owes no such duty.

Assignments should likewise be carefully drawn in order to avoid unnecessary legal disputes. An employee should obtain a written agreement with his employer if possible where his work involves patentable inventions or improvements. Although the employer may not always be in a position to bargain, he should, nevertheless, learn at the outset what his rights are and guide himself accordingly. The exact terms of the contract will depend on whether the employee has been employed to invent a specific thing, or merely to perfect an already existing invention, or to improve it, or to suggest new inventions, or to supervise the work on some invention.

Inventors are required to pay taxes on the income derived from their inventions. An inventor who has some knowledge of the Internal Revenue Code may be able to effect substantial tax savings.

Chapter VII

TRADEMARKS

The trademark is a device used by business enterprise to identify its products and distinguish them from those made or carried by other companies. It may consist of fancy and descriptive words, of pictures, figures, letters, dress labels, business equipment and the like, and a combination of all of these. It may be a business mark, a merchandise mark, or a service mark. It may also be a manufacturer or dealer mark.

Trade names and other symbols such as the appearance of goods are like trademarks if they can be registered as such. Otherwise they can be protected only if the violator's conduct is likely to lead to "passing off," or deceptive presentation.

Historical Development

In medieval times marks designating ownership were an important device. They were not trademarks, but proprietary marks which enabled authorities and especially the guilds to control the trade, and their use as compulsory. Modern parallels are the branding of horses with a proprietary mark and having the distributor's mark blown on bottles used for the distribution of dairy products. In the guild economy the mark was a police mark. The gold-and silversmiths in France and the Italian States, the woolen and linen weavers in England, the hammersmiths in Austria, and most of the guildsmen in Germany were compelled to use a mark to enforce the guild economy.

Constitutional Origin

The protection of the two species of property loosely

referred to as "inventions" and "works of art" is expressly delegated to the federal government in Article I, Section 8 of the United States Constitution:

> The Congress shall have power . . . To promote the Progress of Science and useful Arts, by securing for limited Times to Authors and Inventors the exclusive Right to their respective Writings and Discoveries.

This provision gives rise to both our patent statutes and our copyright statutes. Although the granting of both patents and trademarks is administered by the Patent Office, whereas the registration of copyrights is administered by the Library of Congress, there is no express provision regulating trademarks in the constitution. The federal trademark act stems from the interstate commerce clause, so that there is no exclusivity connected with trademarks. That is, both the states and the federal government may regulate them. On the other hand, patents and copyrights arise from expressly delegated powers. Therefore, the federal government has exclusive jurisdiction in this area.

Acquiring a Trademark

Trademark rights arise out of appropriation and use, and the exclusive right to a particular mark belongs to the one who first appropriates and uses it in connection with a particular business. Registration is merely declaratory of title to the mark and therefore does not affect or perfect the trademark right. While it does confer certain new rights to the mark at the outset, it grants

Trademark Compared to Patents and Copyright

A trademark or service mark is not a government grant, and in this respect is not to be confused with a patent or a copyright. A patent, granted by the government, creates the right to exclude others from practice of an invention. A copyright, issued by the government, creates the right to exclude others from copying a literary or artistic work.

Patents and copyrights are based on the creative efforts of the mind of man. A trademark, on the other hand, is not based on any such thing. It is merely a handy way of identifying goods and a service mark is a handy way of identifying services. The right to use the mark is not granted by the government and registration of a mark in the United States Patent Office does not in itself create any exclusive rights. Rights in a mark are acquired by *use* and use must continue if the rights are to continue. Registration is simply a recognition by the government of the right of the owner to use the mark in commerce to distinguish his goods or services. The invention covered by a patent need never be offered to the public, yet the patent owner is secure in his rights for the term of the grant. A copyrighted work need never be reproduced after the copyright has been acquired, yet the copyright owner is protected for the term of the original grant and during the additional periods for which the renewal is made. The rights in a registered mark, unlike a patent or a copyright, may be forfeited or lost during the term for which the registration was granted.

The Federal Trademark Act of 1905 was the first comprehensive trademark statute. based on the theory that the ownership of a trademark is acquired by adoption and use, registration under the Act merely affected procedural rights. A supplemental Act in 1920 extended the substantive rights conferred by the ten-year clause. This clause permitted the registration of marks used exclusively and in good faith for more than ten years prior to the passage of the Act of 1905 even though they could not be registered thereunder, *e.g.,* secondary-meaning marks (those that have lost their primary meanings as descriptive or geographical terms or as surnames and have acquired, by extensive use or advertising, "secondary meanings" with trademark significance). The Act of 1920 was primarily designed to protect American owners of such secondary-meaning marks in those foreign countries in which registration was contingent upon proof of registration in the home country.

The present trademark act , the Lanham Act of 1946, was

designed to consolidate the old Act and its numerous amendments, to eliminate judicial obscurity created by various conflicting and confusing interpretations, to simplify and liberalize registration, to dispense with mere technical prohibitions, and to provide prompt and effective relief against infringement.

The law of trademarks is part of the law of unfair competition, so that a close connection follows between the common law and statutory law.

Under the Lanham Act, the applicant for registration must certify to the date of his first use of the mark in commerce and must also certify that the mark is still in use. Furthermore, the Act introduced a new technique by which inactive marks can be removed from the register. If further conditions affect the duration of registration upon the filing by the registrant of an affidavit within the sixth year following the date of registration, attesting to the fact that the mark is either still in use or that its nonuse is excusable because of special circumstances and not because of any intention to abandon the mark. Similarly, when a registrant after 20 years seeks the renewal of his registration he must file an affidavit stating that the mark is still in use in commerce. Nonuse of a mark for two consecutive years constitutes prima facie evidence of abandonment. Nonuse may under certain circumstances be excused (scarcity of materials, lack of demand, lack of funds, bankruptcy proceedings, reorganization of business, war, accident, et al). The Commissioner of Patents, acting ex officio, is directed to cancel a registration after inexcusable nonuse for six years.

Registration of trademarks rests on both state and federal legislation. Many of the state statutes were primarily designed to protect particular industries, particular articles, labor and fraternal organizations, or various forms of advertisement. The most important provisions provide penal sanctions for unlawful use, imitation and counterfeiting of trademarks, names, labels, wrappers, bottles, boxes, etc. Likewise, such penal sanctions are imposed for using false representations or other fraudulent means to procure registration.

The penalties vary: some statutes declare trademark infringement a misdemeanor, while others only prescribe fines.

State registration secures state jurisdiction over trademark infringement and has evidentiary value. It is probative of the adoption of the mark, constitutes prima facie evidence of ownership, and gives notice to the public, thereby denying the infringer the defense of ignorance of the trademark owner's right.

For purposes of raising revenues, legislation making the state registration mandatory has been proposed, and these bills have suggested that registration in a given state be the sole determinant of ownership. These proposals have been rejected. Federal registration alone is important. The Lanham Act provides for two registers, a principal and a supplemental register.

No action lies for infringement of an unregistered trademark.

Registration on the principal register is equal to knowledge (constructive notice) of the registrant's claim of ownership and prima facie evidence of such ownership and of the validity of the registration. Such registration may, with certain exceptions, become incontestable and entitle the registrant to have the customs authorities stop the importation into the United States of any goods bearing an infringement trademark and to institute all actions based on the registration in the federal courts. Registration on the supplemental register has only this jurisdictional advantage.

Loss of Trademark Rights

The right of the trademark owner to the exclusive use of the mark is terminated or lost:

1. When the mark ceases to be *distinctive*, which may happen when the trade or the consuming public adopts it as the name of the goods dealt in, so that the mark has become generic.

2. When a mark has been assigned without the good-will of a business, the assignment shall not take effect until certain requirements have been satisfied, *e.g.*, the assignee must, not later than six months from the date of the assignment or within an extended period, apply to the registrar for directions with

respect to the advertisement of the assignment. If he fails to do so the registration becomes invalid.

3. When the owner has *abandoned* the mark. A trademark owner may *abandon* his right if he consciously transfers or surrenders his claim to the mark by consenting to its use by others. He may be stopped from challenging the use of his mark by another if, because of his failure to voice timely objection, the junior user developed a trademark in the belief that his use was unobjectionable. The latter may have been unaware of the trademark owner's right, or may have reasonably assumed that the trademark owner's failure to protest signified acquiesence. Mere lapse of time or mere disuse does not establish abandonment. It is necessary to show not only acts indicating a practical abandonment, but an actual intent to abandon. Involuntary disuse, because of scarcity of raw materials, lack of demand or of funds, bankruptcy, war, fire, etc., does not constitute abandonment.

4. When the owner has forfeited his right to be protected against infringement by using the mark deceptively or in a fraudulent trade.

International Agreements

The United States is party to the International Convention for the Protection of industrial property, founded in Paris in 1833, revised in 1900, 1911, 1925 and 1934. The provisions of the convention relate to patents, utility models, industrial designs, *trademark* and other trade designations, and unfair competition, and are designed to assure the nationals of the member nations a certain measure of protection.

But the United States has not acceded to the two Madrid arrangements of 1891, one of which is for the international registration of trademarks and the other for the repression of false indications of origin.

Appendix A

THE 1909 ACT VS. THE 1976 ACT (A COMPARISON)

	Act of March 4, 1909	Act of October 19, 1976
SUBJECT MATTER	Protects "writings" of an author. Writing has been interpreted as requiring fixation in a tangible form and a certain minimum amount of original, creative author- ship. [Section 4]	Protects "original works of authorship which are fixed in a copy (material object, other than a phonorecord, from which the work can be perceived, reproduced, or otherwise communicated, either directly or with the aid of a machine or device) or a phono- record. [Sections 102(a), 301, 101]

1909 Act (continued)

14 classes of works enumerated:

Class A - Books, including composite and cyclopedic works

Class B - Periodicals, in- cluding newspapers

Class C - Lectures, sermons, addresses (prepared for oral delivery)

Class D - Dramatic or dramatico-musical compositions

Class E - Musical compositions

Class F - Maps

Class G - Works of art; models or designs for works of art

Class H - Reproductions of a work of art

Class I - Drawings of plastic works of a scientific or technical character

Class J - Photographs

Class K - Prints and pictorial illustrations including prints or

1976 Act (continued)

7 classes of works enumerated:

(1) literary works

(2) musical works, including any accompanying words

(3) dramatic works, including any accompanying music

(4) pantomimes and choreographic works

(5) pictorial, graphic, and sculptural works

(6) motion pictures and other audio- visual works

(7) sound recordings. [Section 102(a)]

The Register of Copyrights to specify classification for registration purposes only. Classes will be:

Class TX - for claims in nondramatic literary works, other than audiovisual works, expressed in words, numbers or other verbal or numerical symbols or indicia.

Class PA - for claims in musical works, including any accompanying

78

labels used for articles
of merchandise
Class L - Motion picture
photoplays
Class M - Motion-pictures
other than photoplays
Class N - Sound recordings
[Section 5]

words; dramatic works, including any
accompanying music; pantomimes;
choreographic works; and motion
pictures and other audiovisual works.

Class VA - for claims in pictorial,
graphic, and sculptural works.

Class SR - for claims in works
resulting from the fixation of a
series of musical, spoken,
or other sounds, but not including
the sounds accompanying a motion
picture or other audiovisual work.

"New versions"—"compilations,
abridgments, adaptations,
arrangements, dramatizations,
translations or other new
versions when produced
with the consent of the
copyright owner."
[Section 7]

"Compilations and derivative works."
(Derivative work is defined as
every copyrightable work that
employs preexisting material
or data.) Consent of the copyright owner is not a condition of
protection; copyright protection
"does not extend to any part of
the work" in which the pre-
existing material "has been used
unlawfully." [Section 103]

STANDARDS OF
COPYRIGHT-
ABILITY

Product of case law. Work
must represent an appreciable
amount of original, creative
authorship. Original means that
the author produced it by his own
intellectual effort as distinguished
from copying from another.

Legislative reports accompanying
Public Law 94-553 indicate that the
standards of copyrightability remain
unchanged.

	Act of 1909	Act of 1976
ELIGIBILITY	The following works are eligible for copyright protection in the United States:	All unpublished works are eligible for copyright protection in the United States.
	1. Works by United States citizens;	If the work is published, it is eligible for U.S. protection if one of the following applies:
	2. Works by an author who is domiciled in the U.S. on the date of first publication;	1. On the date of first publication, one or more of the authors is a national or domiciliary of the U.S., or is a national or domiciliary of a foreign nation or sovereign authority of a foreign nation that is a party to a copyright treaty of which the U.S. also is a party;
	3. Works by an author who is a citizen of a country with which the U.S. has copyright relations;	
	4. Works first published in a country other than the U.S. that belongs to the Universal Copyright Convention.	2. If on the date of first publication, one or more of the authors is stateless;
	Works by authors that are stateless—status of these works is unclear. Copyright Office registers these claims under its rule of doubt. [Section 9]	3. If the work is first published in the United States or in a foreign nation that on the date of first publication is a part of the Universal Copyright Convention;
		4. If the work comes within the scope of a Presidential proclamation. [Section 104]
OWNERSHIP & TRANSFER OF OWNERSHIP	Copyright vests initially in the author	The original source of ownership is the author. [Section 201(a)]
	Joint works—There is no statutory provisions but courts have held that, in the absence of an agreement to the contrary, joint authors will be deemed as tenants in common. This means that each owns an undivided interest in the entire work and each has an independent right to use or license the entire work. There is no definition of a "joint work" and courts have defined this extremely broadly and eroded the original concept.	"The authors of a joint work are coowners of copyright in the work." [Section 201(a)] A work is defined as joint when the authors collaborate with each other or if each of the authors prepared his or her contribution with the knowledge and intention that it would be merged with the contributions of the other authors as "inseparable or interdependent parts of a unitary whole." [Section 101]

80

	Act of 1909	Act of 1976

OWNERSHIP & TRANSFER OF OWNERSHIP

Act of 1909

Work made for hire--The statute provides "the word 'author' shall include an employer in the case of works made for hire." [Section 26] There is no definition of a work made for hire in the law. Courts, however, have generally said a work prepared by employee within the scope of his employment is a work made for hire. Important factors include the right of the employer to direct and supervise the manner in which the work is performed, payment of wages or other renumeration, and the existence of a contractual arrangement concerning the creation of the work. Many "commissioned" works have been considered works made for hire.

Copyright said to be indivisible; transfer of anything less than all of the rights was a license. Only transfers of ownership (assignments) had to be in writing and be signed by the party granting the transfer. [Section 28] Assignments should have been recorded in the Copyright Office. [Section 30]

Act of 1976

"In the case of a work made for hire, the employer or other person for whom the work was prepared is considered the author...." [Section 201(b)]

Work made for hire is defined. For a commissioned work or one prepared on special order, only certain categories can be works made for hire. Also, the parties must expressly agree to this in writing and both parties must sign the document. [Section 101]

Copyright is made completely divisible. [Section 201 (d)(2)] Transfer of ownership is defined as an assignment, mortgage, exclusive license of any of the exclusive rights comprised in a copyright, whether limited in time or place of effect. Transfers must be in writing and signed by the party making the transfer. [Section 204] Transfers should be recorded in the Copyright Office. [Section 205]

Transfers made by authors on or after January 1, 1978, otherwise than by will, may be terminated after a certain period of time. The notice of termination must be filed by certain specified people no more than 10 nor less than 2 years before the date of termination. The notice must comply in form, content and manner of service with regulations the Register of Copyrights is to prescribe. [Section 203] Termination of the grant may be effected notwithstanding any agreement to the contrary [Section 203(a)(5)]

81

	Act of 1909	Act of 1976
SECURING COPYRIGHT PROTECTION	For unpublished compositions that are registrable, it is the act of registering a claim in the Copyright Office that secures the copyright. For published works it is the act of publication of the work in visually perceptible copies with the required notice of copyright that secures the copyright. The notice must appear in a location specified by the law, e.g., for a book either upon the title page or the page immediately following. [Section 20] Promptly after publication, a claim should be registered in the Copyright Office. [Section 13] If a work is published without an acceptable notice, copyright protection is lost and cannot be regained.	The act of creation and fixing the work in a copy or phonorecord secures the copyright. [Section 301]
DURATION	For unpublished works the term is exactly 28 years from the date of registration; a renewal claim may be filed in the 28th year in which case there is an additional term of 28 years. Copyright protection will expire either 28 or 56 years from the exact date of registration. For published works the term is same as for unpublished works except the term is measured from the date of first publication. [Section 24]	For works created on or after January 1, 1978, the term of copyright will be: 1. life of the author plus 50 years 2. joint works--life of the last surviving author plus 50 years 3. anonymous, pseudonymous works, if the name of the author is not revealed in Copyright Office records, and works made for hire--100 years from creation or 75 years from first publication, whichever is shorter. [Section 302]

82

	Act of 1909	Act of 1976
DURATION		For unpublished works created, but not registered before January 1, 1978, the term of copyright is the same as for works created after January 1, 1978 except there is a guarantee of protection until December 31, 2002. [Section 303]
		For works under statutory (federal) copyright protection on December 31, 1977--if copyright is renewed during the last (28th) year then the term will be 75 years. [Section 304]
		All terms will run out on December 31st of the year in which they would otherwise expire. [Section 305]
NOTICE WHEN REQUIRED	The required notice of copyright must be affixed to each copy published or offered for sale. [Section 10]	The required notice of copyright must be placed on all visually perceptible copies and phonorecords of sound recordings that are distributed to the public under the authority of the copyright owner. [Sections 401, 402]

83

	Act of 1909	Act of 1976
FORM OF NOTICE	For works other than sound recordings: the word "copyright," the abbreviation "Copr.," or the symbol "©" accompanied by the name of the copyright proprietor and the year in which copyright was secured by publication (or, in some cases, registration). (There are certain exceptions to this basic rule.) [Section 19]	For visually perceptible copies: the symbol © (the letter C in a circle), or the word "copyright," or the abbreviation "Copr."; and the name of the copyright owner, or a recognizable abbreviation or a generally known alternative designation, and the year of first publication. [Section 401]
	For sound recordings: the symbol ℗ (the letter P in a circle), the year of first publication of the sound recording; and the name of the owner of copyright in the sound recording, or a recognizable abbreviation or generally known alternative designation of the name. [Section 19]	For sound recordings: same as the Act of 1909 [Section 402]
PLACEMENT	Specified by type of work — e.g., for a book or other printed publication, upon the title page or the page immediately following....; For music, upon the title page or first page of music...; [Section 20]	For visually perceptible copies — "reasonable notice" of the copyright claim. Copyright Office regulation will include examples of reasonable placement and affixation of the copyright notice. [Section 401]
	For sound recordings — "reasonable notice" of the claim to copyright [Section 20]	For phonorecords of sound recordings — same as the previous law — [Section 402]

84

	Act of 1909	Act of 1976
EFFECT OF OMISSION OR ERROR IN NOTICE	If the notice is omitted or contains a serious error, copyright is lost and cannot be regained.	If the notice is omitted or there is a serious error, there is no effect as long as the claim to copyright is registered in the Copyright Office before or within 5 years of publication without the notice and a "reasonable effort" is made to add the notice to copies that are later distributed in the U.S. [Section 405]
DEPOSIT	"Promptly after publication," two copies of the best edition" are to be deposited with an application and fee of $6.00. Thus, registration and deposit are joined. [Sections 13, 215]	Within three months after the work has been published with a copyright notice in the U.S., the copyright owner should deposit two complete copies or phonorecords of the "best edition". "Best edition" will be determined by the needs of the Library of Congress. The Register of Copyrights, may by regulation, exempt any categories of material from this requirement, or require deposit of only one copy or phonorecord with respect to any category. Alternate forms of deposit may also be allowed. [Section 407]
	Failure to deposit the required material after a "demand" by the Register of Copyrights can result in the copyright becoming void. [Section 14]	Failure to deposit the required material within three months after the Register of Copyrights makes a written demand will subject the copyright owner to fines. [Section 407(d)]
REGISTRATION	Unpublished works that are subject to registration—one complete copy of the work in legible notation must be sent to the Copyright Office with a properly completed application and a fee of $6.00 Phonorecords are not acceptable as deposit copies of the underlying works they embody. [Section 12, 215]	Registration for both published and unpublished works is entirely permissive. There are, however, substantial inducements to register. [Section 408(a)]

Unpublished works—one complete copy or phonorecord must be sent with the appropriate application form and a fee of $10. [Sections 408, 709] |

85

	Act of 1909	Act of 1976
REGISTRATION	Published compositions—two complete copies of the best edition as first published must be sent to the Copyright Office with a properly completed application and a fee of $6.00. The first published edition of a work registered in unpublished form must be registered again. [Sections 12, 13, 215]	Published works—two complete copies of the best edition (or in the case of works first published abroad or contributions to collective works, one complete copy) with an appropriate application and a fee of $10 must be sent to the Copyright Office. [Sections 408, 708]

The Register of Copyrights, by regulation, can require or permit the deposit of identifying material instead of copies, or the deposit of phonorecords rather than notated copies. The Register may also allow the deposit of one copy rather than two and provide for a single registration for a group of related works. [Section 408] |
| COMPULSORY LICENSE TO USE COPYRIGHTED MUSICAL COMPOSITIONS ON PHONORECORDS | The copyright owner of a musical composition has the exclusive right to make or license the first recording of the work.

Whenever the copyright owner of a musical composition has used or permitted his work to be recorded then anyone else may make "similar use" by complying with the compulsory license provisions of the law. | The copyright owner of a musical composition has the exclusive right to make or license the first recording of the work.

Once phonorecords have been distributed to the public in the U.S. under the authority of the copyright owner, the work becomes subject to the compulsory license.

The compulsory license is available only if the user's primary purpose is to distribute the phonorecords to the public for home use. |

86

COMPULSORY LIC-
ENSE TO USE
COPYRIGHTED
MUSICAL COMP-
OSITIONS ON
PHONORECORDS

Compulsory licensee must send to the copyright owner, by registered mail, a notice of his intention to use the music; a copy of that notice must be sent to the Copyright Office for recordation.

Once a copyright owner records or licenses his work for recording, he must file notice of use (Form U) with the Copyright Ofice. Courts have held that the copyright owner cannot collect royalties for any infringing records made before he files this notice [Sections 1(e), 101(e)]

The compulsory license includes the privilege of making a musical arrangement of the work to the extent necessary to conform it to the style or manner of interpretation of the performance involved; the new arrangement cannot change the basic melody or fundamental character of the work. The arrangement is not subject to pro-tection as a derivative work unless the copy-right owner expressly gives his consent.

To obtain a compulsory license, the user must send a notice of his intent to the copyright owner. It must be served before or within 30 days after making and before distributing any phonorecords. This notice must comply in form, content and manner of service with regulations prescribed by the Register of Copy-rights. A copy of this notice need not be sent to the Copyright Office.

To be entitled to royalties the copyright owner must be identified in the registration or other public records of the Copyright Office.

If the registration or other public records of the Copyright Office do not identify the copy-right owner and his address, the notice should be filed with the Copyright Office.

COMPULSORY LIC-
ENSE TO USE
COPYRIGHTED
MUSICAL COMP-
OSITIONS ON
PHONORECORDS

Act of 1909

On the 20th of each month, the compulsory licensee must account to the copyright owner of the music. He must send the required royalty of 2 cents for each "part" manufactured.

Act of 1976

Failure to file a notice of intent forecloses the possibility of a compulsory license.

Compulsory licensee must pay 2 3/4 cents or 1/2 cent per minute of playing time or fraction thereof, whichever is larger, for records that are made and distributed.

Royalty payments are to be made on or before the 20th day of each month. Each payment must be under oath and must comply with the requirements of the Copyright Office regulations.

The Register of Copyrights, by regulation, is to establish criteria for the detailed annual statements of account which must be certified by an independent Certified Public Accountant.

The notice of use (Form U) is no longer required.
[Section 115]

Appendix B

Text of Lanham Trade-Mark Act

[PUBLIC LAW 489—79TH CONGRESS]

[CHAPTER 540—2D SESSION]

[H. R. 1654]

AN ACT

To provide for the registration and protection of trade-marks used in commerce, to carry out the provisions of certain international conventions, and for other purposes.

Be it enacted by the Senate and House of Representatives of the United States of America in Congress assembled,

TITLE I—THE PRINCIPAL REGISTER

SECTION 1. The owner of a trade-mark used in commerce may register his trade-mark under this Act on the principal register hereby established:

(a) By filing in the Patent Office—

(1) a written application, in such form as may be prescribed by the Commissioner, verified by the applicant, or by a member of the firm or an officer of the corporation or association applying, specifying applicant's domicile and citizenship, the date of applicant's first use of the mark, the date of applicant's first use of the mark in commerce, the goods in connection with which the mark is used and the mode or manner in which the mark is used in connection with such goods, and including a statement to the effect that the person making the verification believes himself, or the firm, corporation, or association in whose behalf he makes the verification, to be the owner of the mark sought to be registered, that the mark is in use in commerce, and that no other person, firm, corporation, or association, to the best of his knowledge and belief, has the right to use such mark in commerce either in the identical form thereof or in such near resemblance thereto as might be calculated to deceive: *Provided,* That in the case of every application claiming concurrent use the applicant

shall state exceptions to his claim of exclusive use, in which he shall specify, to the extent of his knowledge, any concurrent use by others, the goods or services in connection with which and the areas in which each concurrent use exists, the periods of each use, and the goods and area for which the applicant desires registration;

(2) a drawing of the mark; and

(3) such number of specimens or facsimiles of the mark as actually used as may be required by the Commissioner.

(b) By paying into the Patent Office the filing fee.

(c) By complying with such rules or regulations, not inconsistent with law, as may be prescribed by the Commissioner.

(d) If the applicant is not domiciled in the United States he shall designate by a written document filed in the Patent Office the name and address of some person resident in the United States on whom may be served notices or process in proceedings affecting the mark. Such notices or process may be served upon the person so designated by leaving with him or mailing to him a copy thereof at the address specified in the last designation so filed. If the person so designated cannot be found at the address given in the last designation, such notice or process may be served upon the Commissioner.

MARKS REGISTRABLE ON THE PRINCIPAL REGISTER

SEC. 2. No trade-mark by which the goods of the applicant may be distinguished from the goods of others shall be refused registration on the principal register on account of its nature unless it—

(a) Consists of or comprises immoral, deceptive, or scandalous matter; or matter which may disparage or falsely suggest a connection with persons, living or dead, institutions, beliefs, or national symbols, or bring them into contempt, or disrepute.

(b) Consists of or comprises the flag or coat of arms or other insignia of the United States, or of any State or municipality, or of any foreign nation, or any simulation thereof.

(c) Consists of or comprises a name, portrait, or signature identifying a particular living individual except by his written consent, or the name, signature, or portrait of a deceased President of the United States during the life of his widow, if any, except by the written consent of the widow.

(d) Consists of or comprises a mark which so resembles a mark registered in the Patent Office or a mark or trade name previously used in the United States by another and not abandoned, as to be likely, when applied to the goods of the applicant, to cause confusion or mistake or to deceive purchasers: *Provided,* That the Commissioner may register as concurrent registrations the same or similar marks to more than one registrant when they have become entitled to use such marks as a result of their concurrent lawful use thereof in commerce prior to any of the filing dates of the applications involved and the Commissioner or a court on appeal determines that confusion or mistake or deceit of purchasers is not likely to result from the continued use of said marks under conditions and limitations as to the mode or place of use or the goods in connection with which such registrations may be granted which conditions and limitations shall be prescribed in the grant of the concurrent registrations thereof; and concurrent registrations may be similarly granted by the Commissioner with such conditions and limitations when a court has finally determined that more than one person is entitled to use the same or similar marks in commerce. The Commissioner shall give not less than thirty days' written notice to all applicants, registrants, and users specified by any of the parties concerned of any application for concurrent registration and of the time and place of the hearings thereon. When the Commissioner decides to grant a concurrent registration the proposed registration shall be published in the Official Gazette of the Patent Office and the application shall be subject to opposition as hereinafter provided for other applications to register marks. Concurrent registrations may be ordered by a court in an action under the provisions of section 4915, Revised Statutes, under such conditions and limitations as the court considers proper in accordance herewith.

(e) Consists of a mark which, (1) when applied to the goods of the applicant is merely descriptive or deceptively misdescriptive of them, or (2) when applied to the goods of the applicant is primarily geographically descriptive or deceptively misdescriptive of them, except as indications of regional origin may be registrable under section 4 hereof, or (3) is primarily merely a surname.

(f) Except as expressly excluded in paragraphs (a), (b), (c), and (d) of this section, nothing herein shall prevent the registration of a mark used by the applicant which has become distinctive of the applicant's goods in commerce. The Commissioner may accept as prima facie evidence that the mark has become distinctive, as applied to the applicant's goods in commerce, proof of substantially exclusive and continuous use thereof as a mark by the applicant in commerce for the five years next preceding the date of the filing of the application for its registration.

SERVICE MARKS REGISTRABLE

Sec. 3. Subject to the provisions relating to the registration of trade-marks, so far as they are applicable, service marks used in commerce shall be registrable, in the same manner and with the same effect as are trade-marks, and when registered they shall be entitled to the protection provided herein in the case of trade-marks, except when used so as to represent falsely that the owner thereof makes or sells the goods on which such mark is used. The Commissioner may establish a separate register for such service marks. Applications and procedure under this section shall conform as nearly as practicable to those prescribed for the registration of trade-marks.

COLLECTIVE AND CERTIFICATION MARKS REGISTRABLE

SEC. 4. Subject to the provisions relating to the registration of trade-marks, so far as they are applicable, collective and certification marks, including indications of regional origin used in commerce, shall be registrable under this Act, in the same manner and with the same effect as are trade-marks, by persons, and nations, States, municipalities, and the like, exercising legitimate control over the use of the marks sought to be registered, even though not possessing an industrial or commercial establishment, and when registered they shall be entitled to the protection provided herein in the case of trade-marks, except when used so as to represent falsely that the owner or a user thereof makes or sells the goods or performs the services on or in connection with which such mark is used. The Commissioner may establish a separate register for such collective marks and certification marks Applications and procedure under this section shall conform as nearly as practicable to those prescribed for the registration of trade-marks.

USE BY RELATED COMPANIES

SEC. 5. Where a registered mark or a mark sought to be registered is or may be used legitimately by related companies, such use shall inure to the benefit of the registrant or applicant for registration, and such use shall not affect the validity of such mark or of its registration, provided such mark is not used in such manner as to deceive the public.

DISCLAIMERS

SEC. 6. The Commissioner shall require unregistrable matter to be disclaimed, but such disclaimer shall not prejudice or affect the applicant's or owner's rights then existing or thereafter arising in the disclaimed matter, nor shall such disclaimer prejudice or affect the applicant's or owner's rights of registration on another application of later date if the disclaimed matter has become distinctive of the applicant's or owner's goods or services.

CERTIFICATES

SEC. 7. (a) Certificates of registration of marks registered upon the principal register shall be issued in the name of the United States of America, under the seal of the Patent Office, and shall either be signed by the Commissioner or have his name printed thereon and attested by an assistant commissioner or by one of the law examiners duly designated by the Commissioner, and a record thereof, together with printed copies of the drawing and statement of the applicant, shall be kept in books for that purpose. The certificate shall reproduce the drawing of the mark, contain the statement of the applicant and state that the mark is registered on the principal register under this Act, the date of the first use of the mark, the date of the first use of the mark in commerce, the particular goods or services for which it is registered, the number and date of the registration, the term thereof, the date on which the application for registration was received in the Patent Office, and any conditions and limitations that may be imposed in the grant of the registration.

(b) A certificate of registration of a mark upon the principal register provided by this Act shall be prima facie evidence of the validity of the registration, registrant's ownership of the mark, and of registrant's exclusive right to use the mark in commerce in connection with the goods or services specified in the certificate, subject to any conditions and limitations stated therein.

(c) A certificate of registration of a mark may be issued to the assignee of the applicant, but the assignment must first be recorded in the Patent Office. In case of change of ownership the Commissioner shall, at the request of the owner and upon a proper showing and the payment of the fee herein provided, issue to such assignee a new certificate of registration of the said mark in the name of such assignee, and for the unexpired part of the original period.

(d) At any time, upon application of the registrant and payment of the fee herein provided, the Commissioner may permit any registration in the Patent Office to be surrendered, canceled, or for good cause to be amended, and he may permit any registered mark to be disclaimed in whole or in part: *Provided,* That the registration when so amended shall still contain registrable matter and the mark as amended shall still be registrable as a whole, and that such amendment or disclaimer does not involve such changes in the registration as to alter materially the character of the mark. The Commissioner shall make appropriate entry upon the records of the Patent Office and upon the certificate of registration or, if said certificate is lost or destroyed, upon a certified copy thereof.

(e) Copies of any records, books, papers, or drawings belonging to the Patent Office relating to marks, and copies of certificates of registration, when authenticated by the seal of the Patent Office and certified by the Commissioner, or in his name by a chief of division duly designated by the Commissioner, shall be evidence in all cases wherein the originals would be evidence; and any person making application therefor and paying the fee required by law shall have such copies.

(f) Whenever a material mistake in a registration, incurred through the fault of the Patent Office, is clearly disclosed by the records of the Office a certificate stating the fact and nature of such mistake, signed by the Commissioner and sealed with the seal of the Patent Office, shall be issued without charge and recorded and a printed copy thereof shall be attached to each printed copy of the registration certificate and such corrected certificate shall thereafter have the same effect as if the same had been originally issued in such corrected form, or in the discretion of the Commissioner a new certificate of registration may be issued without charge. All certificates of correction heretofore issued in accordance with the rules of the Patent Office and the registrations to which they are attached shall have the same force and effect as if such certificates and their issue had been specifically authorized by statute.

(g) Whenever a mistake has been made in a registration and a showing has been made that such mistake occurred in good faith through the fault of the applicant, the Commissioner is authorized to issue a certificate of correction or, in his discretion, a new certificate upon the payment of the required fee: *Provided,* That the correction does not involve such changes in the registration as to require republication of the mark.

DURATION

SEC. 8. (a) Each certificate of registration shall remain in force for twenty years: *Provided,* That the registration of any mark under the provisions of this Act shall be canceled by the Commissioner at the end of six years following its date, unless within one year next preceding the expiration of such six years the registrant shall file in the Patent Office an affidavit showing that said mark is still in use or showing that its nonuse is due to special circumstances which excuse such nonuse and is not due to any intention to abandon the mark. Special notice of the requirement for such affidavit shall be attached to each certificate of registration.

(b) Any registration published under the provisions of subsection (c) of section 12 of this Act shall be canceled by the Commissioner at the end of six years after the date of such publication unless within one year next preceding the expiration of such six years the registrant shall file in the Patent Office an affidavit showing that said mark is still in use or showing that its nonuse is due to special circumstances which excuse such nonuse and is not due to any intention to abandon the mark.

(c) The Commissioner shall notify any registrant who files either of the above-prescribed affidavits of his acceptance or refusal thereof and, if a refusal, the reasons therefor.

RENEWAL

SEC. 9. Each registration may be renewed for periods of twenty years from the end of the expiring period upon the filing of an application therefor accompanied by an affidavit by the registrant stating that the mark is still in use in commerce and the payment of the renewal fee required by this Act; and such application may be made at any time within six months before the expiration of the period for which the certificate of registration was issued or renewed, or it may be made within three months after such expiration on payment of the additional fee herein provided.

An applicant for renewal not domiciled in the United States shall be subject to and comply with the provisions of section 1 (d) hereof.

ASSIGNMENT

SEC. 10. A registered mark or a mark for which application to register has been filed shall be assignable with the goodwill of the business in which the mark is used, or with that part of the goodwill of the business connected with the use of and symbolized by the mark, and in any such assignment it shall not be necessary to include the goodwill of the business connected with the use of and symbolized by any other mark used in the business or by the name or style under which the business is conducted: *Provided,* That any assigned registration may be canceled at any time if the registered mark is being used by, or with the permission of, the assignee so as to misrepresent the source of the goods or services in connection with which the mark is used. Assignments shall be by instruments in writing duly executed. Acknowledgment shall be prima facie evidence of the execution of an assignment and when recorded in the Patent Office the record shall be prima facie evidence of execution. An assignment shall be void as against any subsequent purchaser for a valuable consideration without notice, unless it is recorded in the Patent Office within three months after the date thereof or prior to such subsequent purchase. The Commissioner shall keep a separate record of such assignments submitted to him for recording.

An assignee not domiciled in the United States shall be subject to and comply with the provisions of section 1 (d) hereof.

ACKNOWLEDGMENTS AND VERIFICATIONS

SEC. 11. Acknowledgments and verifications required hereunder may be made before any person within the United States authorized by law to administer oaths, or, when made in a foreign country, before any diplomatic or consular officer of the United States or before any official authorized to administer oaths in the foreign country concerned whose authority shall be proved by a certificate of a diplomatic or consular officer of the United States, and shall be valid if they comply with the laws of the state or country where made.

PUBLICATION

SEC. 12. (a) Upon the filing of an application for registration and payment of the fee herein provided, the Commissioner shall refer the application to the examiner in charge of the registration of marks, who shall cause an examination to be made and, if on such examination it shall appear that the applicant is entitled to registration, the Commissioner shall cause the mark to be published in the Official Gazette of the Patent Office.

(b) If the applicant is found not entitled to registration, the examiner shall advise the applicant thereof and of the reasons therefor. The applicant shall have a period of six months in which to reply or amend his application, which shall then be reexamined. This procedure may be repeated until (1) the examiner finally refuses registration of the mark or (2) the applicant fails for a period of six months to reply or amend or appeal, whereupon the application shall be deemed to have been abandoned, unless it can be shown to the satisfaction of the Commissioner that the delay in responding was unavoidable, whereupon such time may be extended.

(c) A registrant of a mark registered under the provisions of the Act of March 3, 1881, or the Act of February 20, 1905, may, at any time prior to the expiration of the registration thereof, upon the payment of the prescribed fee file with the Commissioner an affidavit setting forth those goods stated in the registration on which said mark is in use in commerce and that the registrant claims the benefits of this Act for said mark. The Commissioner shall publish notice thereof with a reproduction of said mark in the Official Gazette, and notify the registrant of such publication and of the requirement for the affidavit of use or nonuse as provided for in subsection (b) of section 8 of this Act. This subsection shall not be subject to the provisions of section 13 of this Act.

OPPOSITION

SEC. 13. Any person who believes that he would be damaged by the registration of a mark upon the principal register may, upon payment of the required fee, file a verified notice of opposition in the Patent Office, stating the grounds therefor, within thirty days after the publication under subsection (a) of section 12 of this Act of the mark sought to be registered. For good cause shown, the time for filing notice of opposition may be extended by the Commissioner, who shall notify the applicant. An unverified opposition may be filed by a duly authorized attorney, but such opposition shall be null and void unless verified by the opposer within a reasonable time after such filing to be fixed by the Commissioner.

CANCELATION

SEC. 14. Any person who believes that he is or will be damaged by the registration of a mark on the principal register established by this Act, or under the Act of March 3, 1881, or the Act of February 20, 1905, may upon the payment of the prescribed fee, apply to cancel said registration—

(a) within five years from the date of the registration of the mark under this Act; or

(b) within five years from the date of the publication under section 12 (c) hereof of a mark registered under the Act of March 3, 1881, or the Act of February 20, 1905; or

(c) at any time if the registered mark becomes the common decriptive name of an article or substance on which the patent has expired, or has been abandoned or its registration was obtained fraudulently or contrary to the provisions of section 4 or of subsections (a), (b), or (c) of section 2 of this Act for a registration hereunder, or contrary to similar prohibitory provisions of said prior Acts for a registration thereunder, or if the registered mark has been assigned and is being used by, or with the permission of, the assignee so as to misrepresent the source of the goods or services in connection with which the mark is used, or if the mark was registered under the Act of March 3, 1881, or the Act of February 20, 1905, and has not been published under the provisions of subsection (c) of section 12 of this Act; or

(d) at any time in the case of a certification mark on the ground that the registrant (1) does not control, or is not able legitimately to exercise control over, the use of such mark, or (2) engages in the production or marketing of any goods or services to which the mark is applied, or (3) permits the use of such mark for other purposes than as a certification mark, or (4) discriminately refuses to certify or to continue to certify the goods or services of any person who maintains the standards or conditions which such mark certifies.

Provided, That the Federal Trade Commission may apply to cancel on the grounds specified in subsections (c) and (d) of this section any mark registered on the principal register established by this Act, and the prescribed fee shall not be required.

SEC. 15. Except on a ground for which application to cancel may be filed at any time under subsections (c) and (d) of section 14 of this Act, and except to the extent, if any, to which the use of a mark registered on the principal register infringes a valid right acquired under the law of any State or Territory by use of a mark or trade name continuing from a date prior to the date of the publication under this Act of such registered mark, the right of the registrant to use such registered mark in commerce for the goods or services on or in connection with which such registered mark has been in continuous use for five consecutive years subsequent to the date of such registration and is still in use in commerce, shall be incontestable: *Provided,* That—

(1) there has been no final decision adverse to registrant's claim of ownership of such mark for such goods or services, or to registrant's right to register the same or to keep the same on the register; and

(2) there is no proceeding involving said rights pending in the Patent Office or in a court and not finally disposed of; and

(3) an affidavit is filed with the Commissioner within one year after the expiration of any such five-year period setting forth those goods or services stated in the registration on or in connection with which such mark has been in continuous use for such five consecutive years and is still in use in commerce, and the other matters specified in subsections (1) and (2) hereof; and

(4) no incontestable right shall be acquired in a mark or trade name which is the common descriptive name of any article or substance, patented or otherwise.

Subject to the conditions above specified in this section, the incontestable right with reference to a mark registered under this Act shall apply to a mark registered under the Act of March 3, 1881, or the Act of February 20, 1905, upon the filing of the required affidavit with the Commissioner within one year after the expiration of any period of five consecutive years after the date of publication of a mark under the provisions of subsection (c) of section 12 of this Act.

The Commissioner shall notify any registrant who files the above-prescribed affidavit of the filing thereof.

INTERFERENCE

SEC. 16. Whenever application is made for the registration of a mark which so resembles a mark previously registered by another, or for the registration of which another has previously made application, as to be likely when applied to the goods or when used in connection with the services of the applicant to cause confusion or mistake or to deceive purchasers, the Commissioner may declare that an interference exists. No interference shall be declared between an application and the registration of a mark the right to the use of which has become incontestable.

SEC. 17. In every case of interference, opposition to registration, application to register as a lawful concurrent user, or application to cancel the registration of a mark, the Commissioner shall give notice to all parties and shall direct the examiner in charge of interferences to determine and decide the respective rights of registration.

SEC. 18. In such proceedings the Commissioner may refuse to register the opposed mark, may cancel or restrict the registration of a registered mark, or may refuse to register any or all of several interfering marks, or may register the mark or marks for the person or persons entitled thereto, as the rights of the parties hereunder may be established in the proceedings: *Provided*, That in the case of the registration of any mark based on concurrent use, the Commissioner shall determine and fix the conditions and limitations provided for in subsection (d) of section 2 of this Act.

SEC. 19. In all inter partes proceedings equitable principles of laches, estoppel, and acquiescence, where applicable may be considered and applied. The provisions of this section shall also govern proceedings heretofore begun in the Patent Office and not finally determined.

SEC. 20. An appeal may be taken to the Commissioner in person from any final decision of the examiner in charge of interferences or of the registration of marks upon the payment of the prescribed fees.

SEC. 21. Any applicant for registration of a mark, party to an interference proceeding, party to an opposition proceeding, party to an application to register as a lawful concurrent user, party to a cancelation proceeding, or any registrant who has filed an affidavit as provided in section 8, who is dissatisfied with the decision of the

Commissioner may appeal to the United States Court of Customs and Patent Appeals or may proceed under section 4915, Revised Statutes, as in the case of applicants for patents, under the same conditions, rules, and procedure as are prescribed in the case of patent appeals or proceedings so far as they are applicable: *Provided*, That any party who is satisfied with the decision of the Commissioner shall, upon the filing of an appeal to the Court of Customs and Patent Appeals by any dissatisfied party, have the right to elect to have all further proceedings under Revised Statutes 4915, by election as provided in Revised Statutes 4911. The Commissioner of Patents shall not be a necessary party to an inter partes proceeding under Revised Statutes 4915, but he shall be notified of the filing of the bill by the clerk of the court in which it is filed and the Commissioner shall have the right to intervene in the action.

REGISTRATION IS NOTICE

SEC. 22. Registration of a mark on the principal register provided by this Act or under the Act of March 3, 1881, or the Act of February 20, 1905, shall be constructive notice of the registrant's claim of ownership thereof.

TITLE II—THE SUPPLEMENTAL REGISTER

SEC. 23. In addition to the principal register, the Commissioner shall keep a continuation of the register provided in paragraph (b) of section 1 of the Act of March 19, 1920, entitled "An Act to give effect to certain provisions of the convention for the protection of trademarks and commercial names, made and signed in the city of Buenos Aires, in the Argentine Republic, August 20, 1910, and for other purposes", to be called the supplemental register. All marks capable of distinguishing applicant's goods or services and not registrable on the principal register herein provided, except those declared to be unregistrable under paragraphs (a), (b), (c) and (d) of section 2 of this Act, which have been in lawful use in commerce by the proprietor thereof upon or in connection with any goods or services for the year preceding the filing of the application may be registered on the supplemental register upon the payment of the prescribed fee and compliance with the provisions of section 1 so far as they are applicable.

Upon the filing of an application for registration on the supplemental register and payment of the fee herein provided the Commissioner shall refer the application to the examiner in charge of the registration of marks, who shall cause an examination to be made and if on such examination it shall appear that the applicant is entitled to registration, the registration shall be granted. If the applicant is found not entitled to registration the provisions of subsection (b) of section 12 of this Act shall apply.

For the purposes of registration on the supplemental register, a mark may consist of any trade-mark, symbol, label, package, configuration of goods, name, word, slogan, phrase, surname, geographical name, numeral, or device or any combination of any of the foregoing, but such mark must be capable of distinguishing the applicant's goods or services.

Upon a proper showing by the applicant that he has begun the lawful use of his mark in foreign commerce and that he requires domestic registration as a basis for foreign protection of his mark, the Commissioner may waive the requirement of a full year's use and may grant registration forthwith.

CANCELATION

Sec. 24. Marks for the supplemental register shall not be published for or be subject to opposition, but shall be published on registration in the Official Gazette of the Patent Office. Whenever any person believes that he is or will be damaged by the registration of a mark on this register he may at any time apply to the Commissioner to cancel such registration. The Commissioner shall refer such application to the examiner in charge of interferences, who shall give notice thereof to the registrant. If it is found after a hearing before the examiner that the registrant was not entitled to register the mark at the time of his application for registration thereof, or that the mark is not used by the registrant or has been abandoned, the registration shall be canceled by the Commissioner.

Sec. 25. The certificates of registration for marks registered on the supplemental register shall be conspicuously different from certificates issued for marks registered on the principal register.

GENERAL PROVISIONS

Sec. 26. The provisions of this Act shall govern so far as applicable applications for registration and registrations on the supplemental register as well as those on the principal register, but applications for and registrations on the supplemental register shall not be subject to or receive the advantages of sections 2(e), 2(f), 7(b), 12(a), 13 to 18, inclusive, 22, 33, and 42 of this Act.

Sec. 27. Registration of a mark on the supplemental register, or under the Act of March 19, 1920, shall not preclude registration by the registrant on the principal register established by this Act.

Sec. 28. Registration on the supplemental register or under the Act of March 19, 1920, shall not be filed in the Department of the Treasury or be used to stop importations.

TITLE III—NOTICE OF REGISTRATION

Sec. 29. Notwithstanding the provisions of section 22 hereof, a registrant of a mark registered under the Act of March 3, 1881, or the Act of February 20, 1905, or on the principal register established by this Act, shall give notice that his mark is registered by displaying with the mark as used the words "Registered in U. S.

Patent Office" or "Reg. U. S. Pat. Off." or the letter R enclosed within a circle, thus   ; and in any suit for infringement under this Act by such a registrant failing so to mark goods bearing the registered mark, or by a registrant under the Act of March 19, 1920, or by the registrant of a mark on the supplemental register provided by this Act no profits and no damages shall be recovered under the provisions of this Act unless the defendant had actual notice of the registration.

TITLE IV—CLASSIFICATION

Sec. 30. The Commissioner shall establish a classification of goods and services, for convenience of Patent Office administration, but not to limit or extend the applicant's rights. The applicant may register his mark in one application for any or all of the goods or services included in one class, upon or in connection with which he is actually using the mark. The Commissioner may issue a single certificate for one mark registered in a plurality of classes upon payment of a fee equaling the sum of the fees for each registration in each class.

TITLE V—FEES AND CHARGES

Sec. 31. The following fees shall be paid to the Patent Office under this Act:

On filing each original application for registration of a mark in each class on either the principal or the supplemental register, $25; on filing each application for renewal in each class, $25; and on filing each application for renewal in each class after expiration of the registration, an additional fee of $5; on filing notice of claim of benefits of this Act for a mark to be published under section 12(c) hereof, $10; on filing notice of opposition or application for cancelation, $25; on appeal from an examiner in charge of the registration of marks to the Commissioner, $25; on appeal from an examiner in charge of interferences to the Commissioner, $25; for issuance of a new certificate of registration following change of ownership of a mark or correction of a registrant's mistake, $10; for certificate of correction of registrant's mistake, $10; for manuscript copies, for every one hundred words or fraction thereof, 10 cents; for comparing other copies, 5 cents for every one hundred words or fraction thereof; for certifying in any case, additional, $1; for each additional registration or application which may be included under a single certificate, 50 cents additional; for filing disclaimer, amendment, surrender, or cancelation after registration, $10.

For abstracts of title: For the search, one hour or less, and certificate, $3; each additional hour or fraction thereof, $1.50; for each brief from the digest of assignments of two hundred words or less, $1.

For certificate that trade-mark has not been registered—search and certificate (for deposit in foreign countries only), $3.

For title reports required for office use, $1.

For a single printed copy of statement and drawing, 10 cents; if certified, for the grant, additional, $1; for the certificate, $1; if renewed, for copy of certificate of renewal, additional, $1.

For photographic copies of records and drawings, the reasonable cost of making them.

For recording every assignment or other paper not exceeding six pages, $3; for each additional two pages or less, $1; for each additional registration or application included, or involved in one writing where more than one is so included or involved, additional, 50 cents.

The Commissioner shall refund fees paid by mistake or in excess.

TITLE VI—REMEDIES

SEC. 32. (1) Any person who shall, in commerce, (a) use, without the consent of the registrant, any reproduction, counterfeit, copy, or colorable imitation of any registered mark in connection with the sale, offering for sale, or advertising of any goods or services on or in connection with which such use is likely to cause confusion or mistake or to deceive purchasers as to the source of origin of such goods or services; or (b) reproduce, counterfeit, copy, or colorably imitate any such mark and apply such reproduction, counterfeit, copy, or colorable imitation to labels, signs, prints, packages, wrappers, receptacles, or advertisements intended to be used upon or in connection with the sale in commerce of such goods or services, shall be liable to a civil action by the registrant for any or all of the remedies hereinafter provided, except that under subsection (b) hereof the registrant shall not be entitled to recover profits or damages unless the acts have been committed with knowledge that such mark is intended to be used to cause confusion or mistake or to deceive purchasers.

(2) Notwithstanding any other provision of this Act, the remedies given to the owner of the right infringed shall be limited as follows: (a) Where an infringer is engaged solely in the business of printing the mark for others and establishes that he was an innocent infringer the owner of the right infringed shall be entitled as against such infringer only to an injunction against future printing; (b) where the infringement complained of is contained in or is part of paid advertising matter in a newspaper, magazine, or other similar periodical the remedies of the owner of the right infringed as against the publisher or distributor of such newspaper, magazine, or other similar periodical shall be confined to an injunction against the presentation of such advertising matter in future issues of such newspapers, magazines, or other similar periodical: *Provided*, That these limitations shall apply only to innocent infringers; (c) injunction relief shall not be available to the owner of the right infringed in respect of an issue of a newspaper, magazine, or other similar periodical containing infringing matter when restraining the dissemination of such infringing matter in any particular issue of such periodical would delay the delivery of such issue after the regular time therefor, and such delay would be due to the method by which publication and distribution of

such periodical is customarily conducted in accordance with sound business practice, and not to any method or device adopted for the evasion of this section or to prevent or delay the issuance of an injunction or restraining order with respect to such infringing matter.

SEC. 33. (a) Any certificate of registration issued under the Act of March 3, 1881, or the Act of February 20, 1905, or of a mark registered on the principal register provided by this Act and owned by a party to an action shall be admissible in evidence and shall be prima facie evidence of registrant's exclusive right to use the registered mark in commerce on the goods or services specified in the certificate subject to any conditions or limitations stated therein, but shall not preclude an opposing party from proving any legal or equitable defense or defect which might have been asserted if such mark had not been registered.

(b) If the right to use the registered mark has become incontestable under section 15 hereof, the certificate shall be conclusive evidence of the registrant's exclusive right to use the registered mark in commerce on or in connection with the goods or services specified in the certificate subject to any conditions or limitations stated therein except when one of the following defenses or defects is established:

(1) That the registration or the incontestable right to use the mark was obtained fraudulently; or

(2) That the mark has been abandoned by the registrant; or

(3) That the registered mark has been assigned and is being used, by or with the permission of the assignee, so as to misrepresent the source of the goods or services in connection with which the mark is used; or

(4) That the use of the name, term, or device charged to be an infringement is a use, otherwise than as a trade or service mark, of the party's individual name in his own business, or of the individual name of anyone in privity with such party, or of a term or device which is descriptive of and used fairly and in good faith only to describe to users the goods or services of such party, or their geographic origin; or

(5) That the mark whose use by a party is charged as an infringement was adopted without knowledge of the registrant's prior use and has been continuously used by such party or those in privity with him from a date prior to the publication of the registered mark under subsection (a) or (c) of section 12 of this Act: *Provided, however,* That this defense or defect shall apply only for the area in which such continuous prior use is proved.

(6) That the mark whose use is charged as an infringement was registered and used prior to the publication under subsection (a) or (c) of section 12 of this Act of the registered mark of the registrant, and not abandoned: *Provided, however,* That this defense or defect shall apply only where the said mark has been published pursuant to subsection (c) of section 12 and shall apply only for the area in which

the mark was used prior to the date of publication of the registrant's mark under subsection (a) or (c) of section 12 of this Act.

(7) That the mark has been or is being used to violate the antitrust laws of the United States.

Sec. 34. The several courts vested with jurisdiction of civil actions arising under this Act shall have power to grant injunctions, according to the principles of equity and upon such terms as the court may deem reasonable, to prevent the violation of any right of the registrant of a mark registered in the Patent Office. Any such injunction may include a provision directing the defendant to file with the court and serve on the plaintiff within thirty days after the service on the defendant of such injunction, or such extended period as the court may direct, a report in writing under oath setting forth in detail the manner and form in which the defendant has complied with the injunction. Any such injunction granted upon hearing, after notice to the defendant, by any district court of the United States, may be served on the parties against whom such injunction is granted anywhere in the United States where they may be found, and shall be operative and may be enforced by proceedings to punish for contempt, or otherwise, by the court by which such injunction was granted, or by any other United States district court in whose jurisdiction the defendant may be found.

The said courts shall have jurisdiction to enforce said injunction, as herein provided, as fully as if the injunction had been granted by the district court in which it is sought to be enforced. The clerk of the court or judge granting the injunction shall, when required to do so by the court before which application to enforce said injunction is made, transfer without delay to said court a certified copy of all papers on file in his office upon which said injunction was granted.

It shall be the duty of the clerks of such courts within one month after the filing of any action, suit, or proceeding arising under the provisions of this Act to give notice thereof in writing to the Commissioner setting forth in order so far as known the names and addresses of the litigants and the designating number or numbers of the registration or registrations upon which the action, suit, or proceeding has been brought, and in the event any other registration be subsequently included in the action, suit, or proceeding by amendment, answer, or other pleading, the clerk shall give like notice thereof to the Commissioner, and within one month after the decision is rendered, appeal taken or a decree issued the clerk of the court shall give notice thereof to the Commissioner, and it shall be the duty of the Commissioner on receipt of such notice forthwith to endorse the same upon the file wrapper of the said registration or registrations and to incorporate the same as a part of the contents of said file wrapper.

Sec. 35. When a violation of any right of the registrant of a mark registered in the Patent Office shall have been established in any civil action arising under this Act, the plaintiff shall be entitled, subject to the provisions of sections 29 and 31 (1) (b), and subject to the principles of equity, to recover (1) defendant's profits, (2) any damages sustained by the plaintiff, and (3) the costs of the action. The court shall assess such profits and damages or cause the same to be assessed under its direction. In assessing profits the plaintiff shall be required to prove defendant's sales only; defendant must prove all elements of cost or deduction claimed. In assessing damages the court may enter judgment, according to the circumstances of the case, for any sum above the amount found as actual damages, not exceeding three times such amount. If the court shall find that the amount of the recovery based on profits is either inadequate or excessive the court may in its discretion enter judgment for such sum as the court shall find to be just, according to the circumstances of the case. Such sum in either of the above circumstances shall constitute compensation and not a penalty.

SEC. 36. In any action arising under this Act, in which a violation of any right of the registrant of a mark registered in the Patent Office shall have been established, the court may order that all labels, signs, prints, packages, wrappers, receptacles, and advertisements in the possession of the defendant, bearing the registered mark or any reproduction, counterfeit, copy, or colorable imitation thereof, and all plates, molds, matrices, and other means of making the same, shall be delivered up and destroyed.

SEC. 37. In any action involving a registered mark the court may determine the right to registration, order the cancelation of registrations, in whole or in part, restore canceled registrations, and otherwise rectify the register with respect to the registrations of any party to the action. Decrees and orders shall be certified by the court to the Commissioner, who shall make appropriate entry upon the records of the Patent Office, and shall be controlled thereby.

SEC. 38. Any person who shall procure registration in the Patent Office of a mark by a false or fraudulent declaration or representation, oral or in writing, or by any false means, shall be liable in a civil action by any person injured thereby for any damages sustained in consequence thereof.

SEC. 39. The district and territorial courts of the United States shall have original jurisdiction, the circuit courts of appeals of the United States and the United States Court of Appeals for the District of Columbia shall have appellate jurisdiction, of all actions arising under this Act, without regard to the amount in controversy or to diversity or lack of diversity of the citizenship of the parties.

SEC. 40. Writs of certiorari may be granted by the Supreme Court of the United States for the review of cases arising under this Act in the same manner as provided for in cases under the patent laws.

SEC. 41. The Commissioner shall make rules and regulations, not inconsistent with law, for the conduct of proceedings in the Patent Office under this Act.

TITLE VII—IMPORTATION FORBIDDEN OF GOODS BEARING INFRINGING MARKS OR NAMES

SEC. 42. That no article of imported merchandise which shall copy or simulate the name of any domestic manufacture, or manufacturer, or trader, or of any manufacturer or trader located in any foreign country which, by treaty, convention, or law affords similar privileges to citizens of the United States, or which shall copy or simulate a trade-mark registered in accordance with the provisions of this Act or shall bear a name or mark calculated to induce the public to believe that the article is manufactured in the United States, or that it is manufactured in any foreign country or locality other than the country or locality in which it is in fact manufactured, shall be admitted to entry at any customhouse of the United States; and, in order to aid the officers of the customs in enforcing this prohibition, any domestic manufacturer or trader, and any foreign manufacturer or trader, who is entitled under the provisions of a treaty, convention, declaration, or agreement between the United States and any foreign country to the advantages afforded by law to citizens of the United States in respect to trade-marks and commercial names, may require his name and residence, and the name of the locality in which his goods are manufactured, and a copy of the certificate of registration of his trade-mark, issued in accordance with the provisions of this Act, to be recorded in books which shall be kept for this purpose in the Department of the Treasury, under such regulations as the Secretary of the Treasury shall prescribe, and may furnish to the Department facsimiles of his name, the name of the locality in which his goods are manufactured, or of his registered trade-mark, and thereupon the Secretary of the Treasury shall cause one or more copies of the same to be transmitted to each collector or other proper officer of customs.

TITLE VIII—FALSE DESIGNATIONS OF ORIGIN AND FALSE DESCRIPTIONS FORBIDDEN

SEC. 43. (a) Any person who shall affix, apply, or annex, or use in connection with any goods or services, or any container or containers for goods, a false designation of origin, or any false description or representation, including words or other symbols tending falsely to describe or represent the same, and shall cause such goods or services to enter into commerce, and any person who shall with knowledge of the falsity of such designation of origin or description or representation cause or procure the same to be transported or used in commerce or deliver the same to any carrier to be transported or used, shall be liable to a civil action by any person doing business in the locality falsely indicated as that of origin or in the region in which said locality is situated, or by any person who believes that he is or is likely to be damaged by the use of any such false description or representation.

(b) Any goods marked or labeled in contravention of the provisions of this section shall not be imported into the United States or admitted to entry at any customhouse of the United States. The owner, importer, or consignee of goods refused entry at any customhouse under this section may have any recourse by protest or appeal that is given under the customs revenue laws or may have the remedy given by this Act in cases involving goods refused entry or seized.

TITLE IX—INTERNATIONAL CONVENTIONS

SEC. 44. (a) The Commissioner shall keep a register of all marks communicated to him by the international bureaus provided for by the conventions for the protection of industrial property, trade-marks, trade and commercial names, and the repression of unfair competition to which the United States is or may become a party, and upon the payment of the fees required by such conventions and the fees herein prescribed may place the marks so communicated upon such register. This register shall show a facsimile of the mark or trade or commercial name; the name, citizenship, and address of the registrant; the number, date, and place of the first registration of the mark, including the dates on which application for such registration was filed and granted and the term of such registration; a list of goods or services to which the mark is applied as shown by the registration in the country of origin, and such other data as may be useful concerning the mark. This register shall be a continuation of the register provided in section 1 (a) of the Act of March 19, 1920.

(b) Persons who are nationals of, domiciled in, or have a bona fide and effective business or commercial establishment in any foreign country, which is a party to (1) the International Convention for the Protection of Industrial Property, signed at Paris on March 20, 1883; or (2) the General Inter-American Convention for Trade Mark and Commercial Protection signed at Washington on February 20, 1929; or (3) any other convention or treaty relating to trade-marks, trade or commercial names, or the repression of unfair competition to which the United States is a party, shall be entitled to the benefits and subject to the provisions of this Act to the extent and under the conditions essential to give effect to any such conventions and treaties so long as the United States shall continue to be a party thereto, except as provided in the following paragraphs of this section.

(c) No registration of a mark in the United States by a person described in paragraph (b) of this section shall be granted until such mark has been registered in the country of origin of the applicant, unless the applicant alleges use in commerce.

For the purposes of this section, the country of origin of the applicant is the country in which he has a bona fide and effective industrial or commercial establishment, or if he has not such an establishment the country in which he is domiciled, or if he has not a domicile in any of the countries described in paragraph (b) of this section, the country of which he is a national.

(d) An application for registration of a mark under sections 1, 2, 3, 4, or 23 of this Act filed by a person described in paragraph (b) of this section who has previously duly filed an application for registration of the same mark in one of the countries described in paragraph (b) shall be accorded the same force and effect as would be accorded to the same application if filed in the United States on the same date on which the application was first filed in such foreign country: *Provided*, That—

(1) the application in the United States is filed within six months from the date on which the application was first filed in the foreign country;

(2) the application conforms as nearly as practicable to the requirements of this Act, but use in commerce need not be alleged;

(3) the rights acquired by third parties before the date of the filing of the first application in the foreign country shall in no way be affected by a registration obtained on an application filed under this subsection (d);

(4) nothing in this subsection (d) shall entitle the owner of a registration granted under this section to sue for acts committed prior to the date on which his mark was registered in this country unless the registration is based on use in commerce.

(e) A mark duly registered in the country of origin of the foreign applicant may be registered on the principal register if eligible, otherwise on the supplemental register herein provided. The application therefor shall be accompanied by a certified copy of the application for or registration in the country of origin of the applicant.

(f) The registration of a mark under the provisions of paragraphs (c), (d), and (e) of this section by a person described in paragraph (b) shall be independent of the registration in the country of origin and the duration, validity, or transfer in the United States of such registration shall be governed by the provisions of this Act.

(g) Trade names or commercial names of persons described in paragraph (b) of this section shall be protected without the obligation of filing or registration whether or not they form parts of marks.

(h) Any person designated in paragraph (b) of this section as entitled to the benefits and subject to the provisions of this Act shall be entitled to effective protection against unfair competition, and the remedies provided herein for infringement of marks shall be available so far as they may be appropriate in repressing acts of unfair competition.

(i) Citizens or residents of the United States shall have the same benefits as are granted by this section to persons described in paragraph (b) hereof.

TITLE X—CONSTRUCTION AND DEFINITIONS

SEC. 45. In the construction of this Act, unless the contrary is plainly apparent from the context—

The United States includes and embraces all territory which is under its jurisdiction and control.

The word "commerce" means all commerce which may lawfully be regulated by Congress.

The term "principal register" refers to the register provided for by sections 1 through 22 hereof, and the term "supplemental register" refers to the register provided for by sections 23 through 28 hereof.

The term "person" and any other word or term used to designate the applicant or other entitled to a benefit or privilege or rendered liable under the provisions of this Act includes a juristic person as well as a natural person. The term "juristic person" includes a firm, corporation, union, association, or other organization capable of suing and being sued in a court of law.

The terms "applicant" and "registrant" embrace the legal representatives and successors and assigns of such applicant or registrant.

The term "Commissioner" means the Commissioner of Patents.

The term "related company" means any person who legitimately controls or is controlled by the registrant or applicant for registration in respect to the nature and quality of the goods or services in connection with which the mark is used.

The terms "trade name" and "commercial name" include individual names and surnames, firm names and trade names used by manufacturers, industrialists, merchants, agriculturists, and others to identify their businesses, vocations, or occupations; the names or titles lawfully adopted and used by persons, firms, associations, corporations, companies, unions, and any manufacturing, industrial, commercial agricultural, or other organizations engaged in trade or commerce and capable of suing and being sued in a court of law.

The term "trade-mark" includes any word, name, symbol, or device or any combination thereof adopted and used by a manufacturer or merchant to identify his goods and distinguish them from those manufactured or sold by others.

The term "service mark" means a mark used in the sale or advertising of services to identify the services of one person and distinguish them from the services of others and includes without limitation the marks, names, symbols, titles, designations, slogans, character names, and distinctive features of radio or other advertising used in commerce.

The term "certification mark" means a mark used upon or in connection with the products or services of one or more persons other than the owner of the mark to certify regional or other origin, material, mode of manufacture, quality, accuracy or other characteristics of such goods or services or that the work or labor on the goods or services was performed by members of a union or other organization.

The term "collective mark" means a trade-mark or service mark used by the members of a cooperative, an association or other collective group or organization and includes marks used to indicate membership in a union, an association or other organization.

The term "mark" includes any trade-mark, service mark, collective mark, or certification mark entitled to registration under this Act whether registered or not.

For the purposes of this Act a mark shall be deemed to be used in commerce (a) on goods when it is placed in any manner on the goods or their containers or the displays associated therewith or on the tags or labels affixed thereto and the goods are sold or transported in commerce and (b) on services when it is used or displayed in the sale or advertising of services and the services are rendered in commerce.

A mark shall be deemed to be "abandoned"—

(a) When its use has been discontinued with intent not to resume. Intent not to resume may be inferred from circumstances. Nonuse for two consecutive years shall be prima facie abandonment.

(b) When any course of conduct of the registrant, including acts of omission as well as commission, causes the mark to lose its significance as an indication of origin.

The term "colorable imitation" includes any mark which so resembles a registered mark as to be likely to cause confusion or mistake or to deceive purchasers.

The term "registered mark" means a mark registered in the United States Patent Office under this Act or under the Act of March 3, 1881, or the Act of February 20, 1905, or the Act of March 19, 1920. The phrase "marks registered in the Patent Office" means registered marks.

The term "Act of March 3, 1881", "Act of February 20, 1905", or "Act of March 19, 1920", means the respective Act as amended.

A "counterfeit" is a spurious mark which is identical with, or substantially indistinguishable from, a registered mark.

Words used in the singular include the plural and vice versa.

The intent of this Act is to regulate commerce within the control of Congress by making actionable the deceptive and misleading use of marks in such commerce; to protect registered marks used in such commerce from interference by State, or territorial legislation; to protect persons engaged in such commerce against unfair competition; to prevent fraud and deception in such commerce by the use of reproductions, copies, counterfeits, or colorable imitations of registered marks; and to provide rights and remedies stipulated by treaties and conventions respecting trade-marks, trade names, and unfair competition entered into between the United States and foreign nations.

TITLE XI—REPEAL OF PREVIOUS ACTS

Sec. 46. (a) This Act shall be in force and take effect one year from its enactment, but except as otherwise herein specifically provided shall not affect any suit, proceeding, or appeal then pending. All Acts and parts of Acts inconsistent herewith are hereby repealed effective one year from the enactment hereof, including the following Acts insofar as they are inconsistent herewith: The Act of Congress approved March 3, 1881, entitled "An Act to authorize the registration of trade-marks and protect the same"; the Act approved August 5, 1882, entitled "An Act relating to the registration of trade-marks"; the Act of February 20, 1905 (U. S. C., title 15, secs. 81 to 109, inclusive), entitled "An Act to authorize the registration of trade-marks used in commerce with foreign nations or among the several States or with Indian tribes, and to protect the same", and the amendments thereto by the Acts of May 4, 1906 (U. S. C., title 15, secs. 131 and 132; 34 Stat. 169), March 2, 1907 (34 Stat. 1251, 1252), February 18, 1909 (35 Stat. 627, 628), February 18, 1911 (36 Stat. 918), January 8, 1913 (37 Stat. 649), June 7, 1924 (43 Stat. 647) March 4, 1925 (43 Stat. 1268, 1269), April 11, 1930 (46 Stat. 155), June 10, 1938 (Public Numbered 586, Seventy-fifth Congress, ch. 332 third session); the Act of March 19 1920 (U. S. C., title 15, secs. 121 to 128, inclusive), entitled "An Act to give effect to certain provisions of the convention for the protection of trade-marks and commercial names made and signed in the city of Buenos Aires, in the Argentine Republic, August 20, 1910, and for other purposes", and the amendments thereto, including the Act of June 10, 1938 (Public, Numbered 586, Seventy-fifth Congress, ch. 332, third session): *Provided*, That this repeal shall not affect the validity of registrations granted or applied for under any of said Acts prior to the effective date of this Act, or rights or remedies thereunder except as provided in sections 8, 12, 14, 15, and 47 of this Act; but nothing contained in this Act shall be construed as limiting, restricting, modifying, or repealing any statute in force on the effective date of this Act which does not relate to trade-marks, or as restricting or increasing the authority of any Federal department or regulatory agency except as may be specifically provided in this Act.

(b) Registrations now existing under the Act of March 3, 1881, or the Act of February 20, 1905, shall continue in full force and effect for the unexpired terms thereof and may be renewed under the provisions of section 9 of this Act. Such registrations and the renewals thereof shall be subject to and shall be entitled to the benefits of the provisions of this Act to the same extent and with the same force and effect as though registered on the principal register established by this Act except as limited in sections 8, 12, 14, and 15 of this Act. Marks registered under the "ten-year proviso" of section 5 of the Act of February 20, 1905, as amended, shall be deemed to have become distinctive of the registrant's goods in commerce under paragraph (f) of section 2 of this Act and may be renewed under section 9 hereof as marks coming within said paragraph.

Registrations now existing under the Act of March 19, 1920, shall expire six months after the effective date of this Act, or twenty years from the dates of their registrations, whichever date is later. Such registrations shall be subject to and entitled to the benefits of the provisions of this Act relating to marks registered on the supplemental register established by this Act, and may not be renewed unless renewal is required to support foreign registrations. In that event renewal may be effected on the supplemental register under the provisions of section 9 of this Act.

Marks registered under previous Acts may, if eligible, also be registered under this Act.

Sec. 47. (a) All applications for registration pending in the Patent Office at the effective date of this Act may be amended, if practicable, to bring them under the provisions of this Act. The prosecution of such applications so amended and the grant of registrations thereon shall be proceeded with in accordance with the provisions of this Act. If such amendments are not made, the prosecution of said applications shall be proceeded with and registrations thereon granted in accordance with the Acts under which said applications were filed, and said acts are hereby continued in force to this extent and for this purpose only, notwithstanding the foregoing general repeal thereof.

(b) In any case in which an appeal is pending before the United States Court of Customs and Patent Appeals or any United States Circuit Court of Appeals or the United States Court of Appeals for the District of Columbia or the United States Supreme Court at the effective date of this Act, the court, if it be of the opinion that the provisions of this Act are applicable to the subject matter of the appeal, may apply such provision or may remand the case to the Commissioner or to the district court for the taking of additional evidence or a new trial or for reconsideration of the decision on the record as made, as the appellate court may deem proper.

Sec. 48. Section 4 of the Act of January 5, 1905 (U. S. C., title 36, sec. 4), as amended, entitled "An Act to incorporate the National Red Cross", and section 7 of the Act of June 15, 1916 (U. S. C., title 36, sec. 27), entitled "An Act to incorporate the Boy Scouts of America, and for other purposes", and the Act of June 20, 1936 (U. S. C., title 22, sec. 248), entitled "An Act to prohibit the commercial use of the coat of arms of the Swiss Confederation", are not repealed or affected by this Act.

Sec. 49. Nothing herein shall adversely affect the rights or the enforcement of rights in marks acquired in good faith prior to the effective date of this Act.

Sec. 50. If any provision of this Act or the application of such provision to any person or circumstance is held invalid, the remainder of the Act shall not be affected thereby.

Approved July 5, 1946.

Appendix C

EXAMPLE OF TWO PATENT APPLICATIONS DESCRIBING SIMILAR "INVENTIONS"

Patented Oct. 25, 1932

1,884,238

UNITED STATES PATENT OFFICE

FREDERICK R. REUTTER, OF WATERBURY, CONNECTICUT, ASSIGNOR TO SCOVILL MANUFACTURING COMPANY, OF WATERBURY, CONNECTICUT, A CORPORATION OF CONNECTICUT

HUB CAP

Application filed July 11, 1930. Serial No. 467,349.

This invention relates to improvements in hub caps and especially to automobile hub caps.

The object of the invention is to provide an improved hub cap which is readily and cheaply manufactured, attractive in appearance and readily attached and detached.

In the accompanying drawing forming a part of this specification, there is shown by way of illustration a construction embodying all the features of the invention in its preferred form and this construction will now be described in detail and the features forming the invention then specifically pointed out in the claims.

In the drawing:

Figure 1 is a top plan view of the cap partially broken away to show its construction;

Figure 2 is a sectional view on line 2—2 of Figure 1 and

Figure 3 is a partial sectional view of a modification.

The hub cap comprises a body portion made of sheet metal circular in shape and somewhat disk shaped and has extending substantially at right angles thereto a flange adapted to enter the rim of the automobile hub, this flange preferably being inset from the outer edge of the body portion so that the body portion covers the hub rim when in position on the hub. Extending over the body member and of the same general shape, is an ornamental plate, which is retained in position by bending its outer periphery over the outer periphery of the body member.

Referring to the construction shown in the drawing, the body member is shown as comprising a cap plate 1 and a flanged plate 2 bent outwardly and shaped to lie against the inner side of the outer periphery of the cap plate 1 to form therewith a bead 3 over which the outer periphery of the ornamental plate 4 is bent to firmly and securely hold the parts together. The center of the ornamental plate 4 is provided with a hole 5 in back of which is a design plate 6, the edges of which fit between the ornamental plate 4 and the cap plate 1 so as to be supported by the plates 4, 1 and securely held in position thereby. If desired, the design plate may be secured to the body plate by rivets 7, as shown in Figure 3, to hold the design plate in circumferential position.

The hub cap is secured to the automobile hub by suitable latch devices which preferably are of the form shown. The flange 2 is upset or punched inwardly to form recesses in its outer surface on each of which rivets 8 hold a spring plate 9 on the inner side of flange 2. The opposite end of the spring plate 9 has secured thereto a conical nib 10 which projects through a suitable opening 11 in the flange 2, the nib 10 being adapted to snap into and out of engagement with suitable openings in the automobile hub rim.

It will be understood that the construction may be modified within the invention as defined by the claims.

What is claimed is:

1. In a hub cap, a body member, means on said body member for engaging a hub, an ornamental plate for said body member, said ornamental plate having a hole therein, and a design plate behind said hole and supported by said body member and said ornamental plate.

2. In a hub cap, a body member having an inwardly directed hub engaging flange forming with the body member a circumferential bead, an ornamental plate for said body member having its edges turned over in engagement with said bead, said ornamental plate having a hole therein, and a design plate back of said hole and supported by said body member and said ornamental plate.

3. In a hub cap, a body member turned over and in to form a circumferential bead and a hub engaging flange, means attached to said body member and extending through said flange to lock the cap to the hub, an ornamental plate for said body member having its edges turned over in engagement with said bead, said ornamental plate having a hole therein, and a design plate back of said hole and supported by said body member and said ornamental plate.

In testimony whereof, I have hereunto set my hand.

FREDERICK R. REUTTER.

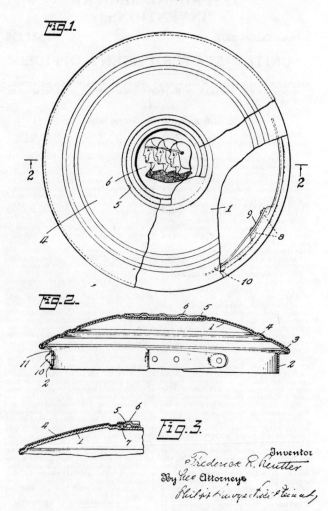

Fig.1.

Fig.2.

Fig.3.

Inventor

Frederick R. Reutter

By his Attorneys

Philip Hanford Smith & Steinach

UNITED STATES PATENT OFFICE

2,130,220

NONROTATABLE HUB CAP

George D. Ball and Charles L. Tumulty, Alexandria, Ind.

Application October 8, 1937, Serial No. 167,944

9 Claims. (Cl. 40—129)

This invention relates to a non-rotatable hub cap structure.

The chief object of this invention is to provide a hub cap structure which may be readily substituted for a standard, normally rotatable, hub cap and when substituted includes a normally non-rotatable cover arrangement which fully conceals all rotatable parts thereof and of the supporting hub as well.

The chief feature of the invention is the arrangement and construction of the device whereby the foregoing object is accomplished.

Other objects and features will appear more fully hereinafter.

The full nature of the invention will be understood from the accompanying drawing and the following description and claims:

In the drawing, Fig. 1 is a central sectional view through one embodiment of the hub cap structure, including the invention.

Fig. 2 is a front view thereof.

In Fig. 1 of the drawing, there is illustrated a base plate 10 of dished formation having its peripheral edge 11 turned back and beaded as at 12. Suitably secured to the inside of this plate as by welding or the like, is a sleeve portion 13, the projecting edge 14 of which is turned back to form a beaded arrangement 15. The parts thus described are substantially identical to parts of a standard hub cap structure, it being understood for the purpose of disclosing this invention, the plate 10 has covering the same an outer cover plate of suitable ornamented design, the same being rigidly secured to said base plate at its periphery by being crimped or curled around the beaded edge 12.

This standard hub cover cap is frictionally associated with the wheel hub structure through the sleeve portion 13. This is conventional practice and is merely set forth herein for an understanding of the invention, it being understood thereby that the mounting of the structure upon the wheel hub is through the portion 13 in the conventional manner and, therefore, the portion 13 and the supporting base 10 rotate with the wheel hub.

The present invention is arranged to utilize these standard portions but in place of having the cover plate before mentioned rigidly secured to the base plate 10, there is now provided a cover plate 16 which has its peripheral edge 17 turned inwardly as at 18 and masks but is disassociated from the edge 11—12 of the base plate. This cover structure may be suitably ornamented and have a suitable central formation. Herein it is provided with a central well portion 19. This well portion may be a continuation of the portion 16 or may be of a detachable insert character. It may be suitably ornamented.

A sleeve 20 includes near one end an exterior groove 21 and the portion 19 or the portion 16, if desired, includes suitable anchoring means, herein shown in the form of clips 22 welded to the portion 19 and having the finger portions 22a seatable in the groove. Through this arrangement, the cover cap 16 is rigidly associated with the sleeve 20. Any other suitable connection may be provided, however. The reason for this type of connection is that the parts 16 and 13 together with the parts hereinafter to be described may be fabricated in mass production for a large variety of vehicles and only the portion 16, as desired, may be utilized.

The sleeve 20 is provided with two spaced internal grooves 23 and 24. Split locking rings 25 and 26 respectively, retain in the sleeve 20 against axial displacement, an anti-friction structure indicated generally by the numeral 27, the outer sleeve portion 28 of which is relatively rigid with the sleeve 20 and the inner sleeve portion 29 of which is rotatable relative thereto by reason of the balls 30.

A spindle 31 having the head portion 32 extends through and bears against, respectively, the inner raceway portion 29. A spacing sleeve structure 33 bears against the opposite face of the inner raceway member 29 and serves as a spacer to position the race structure in predetermined position on the spindle 31 relative to the plate 10. The spacing sleeve or collar 33 may be enlarged laterally as at 34 to provide a greater area in contact with the sheet metal base plate 10.

The base plate 10 is apertured as at 35 and the same registers with a threaded opening 36 in the spindle 31. A relatively large washer 37 is positioned on the opposite side of the base plate 10 and the cap screw 38 extends through the washer 37, the aperture 35 in the base plate 10, and is threaded into the threaded opening 36 of the spindle 31. This rigidly connects the spindle structure to a base plate 10 and by reason of the spacing sleeve 33—34 and the head portion 32, the anti-friction structure is positively positioned with respect to the base plate in connection with axial displacement. Thus, the interior end of the sleeve 20 is maintained out of contact with the base plate 10 so that the entire masking or cover structure has no contact with the base plate 10 and is relatively rotatably supported with respect thereto, it, of course, being understood that in op-

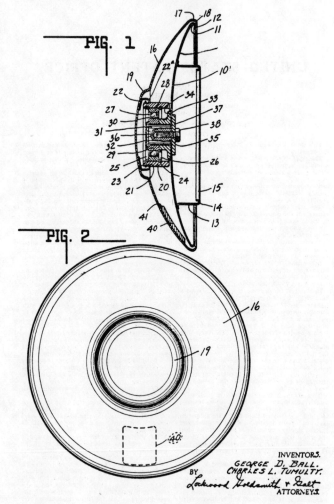

FIG. 1

FIG. 2

INVENTORS.
GEORGE D. BALL.
CHARLES L. TUMULTY.
BY Lockwood Goldsmith & Galt
ATTORNEYS.

116

INDEX

118

LEGAL ALMANAC SERIES CONVERSION TABLE
List of Original Titles and Authors

LEGAL ALMANAC SERIES CONVERSION TABLE
List of Present Titles and Authors